The Story of Romance & Courage in the Life of

ANDRE THORNTON

as Told to Al Janssen

TRIUMPH
BORN OF
TRAGEDY

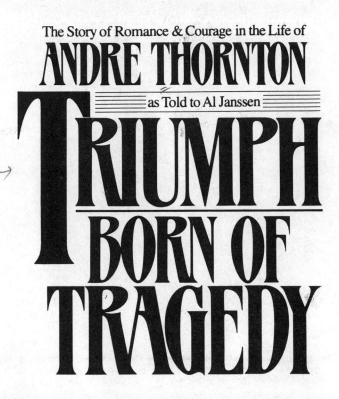

HARVEST HOUSE PUBLISHERS
Eugene, Oregon 97402

TRIUMPH BORN OF TRAGEDY

In Loving Memory of

Gertrude Thomas Thornton

Dedication

My parents, Harold and Arcola Thornton, for their love and support throughout the years, and especially in my time of greatest need.

James and Hazel Thomas, who by their example taught me much about how to love.

Two special women, Gert and Gail. Few men ever have the privilege of knowing one, much less two such wonderful women.

Foreword

If you think this book will take you to the ball park, you are in for a surprise. Yes, it is about a professional baseball player, and he plays in the major leagues. He hits home runs—plenty of them. However, he is more interested in getting other people a home in heaven. He is more interested in keeping other people out of hell than in getting them out at first base. He has heard the roar of the fans, but he wants the approval of Christ. This is the true story of what God has done and is doing in the life of Andre Thornton.

My first contact with Andre Thornton was when he wrote me a letter telling me that he was listening to my radio program, "Through the Bible." At the time, he was in the minor leagues, and he had started listening to the program through the influence of his mother.

We corresponded quite a bit and I finally met Andre in 1974, his first full season in the major leagues. His Chicago Cubs team was playing in Los Angeles and he drove out to meet me at my office. I was pleased to discover that this young man was a very serious student of the Bible, and desired to learn and grow in his faith. It is an attitude I have rarely seen among men of athletic fame.

Then tragedy struck. In the ensuing months I was able to watch how God can sustain a person through the most painful loss. Through tragedy, God lifted Andre to a new understanding of divine love and purpose.

I heartily recommend this book. It is a testimony of the power of God's Word in the life of one man. And I wait in happy anticipation for the next chapter in Andre's thrilling encounter with Jesus Christ in His service.

—Dr. J. Vernon McGee

Preface

In October of 1977, a tragic accident occurred in my life. It was something that has overshadowed my career as a major league baseball player. In the months and years that followed, I have received thousands of letters from people all over the country. Many of them have asked me how I was able to cope with such a tragedy. They wanted answers to difficult questions about life and death. They wanted to know about the hope I cling to.

Because of the sheer volume of mail, it has been impossible for me to personally answer every letter. So in a way, this book is my answer to those who wrote, and to many others who read about my trials and prayed for me and offered their encouragement. It is my hope that this book will answer many of the questions I have been asked. I hope you will find it an encouragement and help. My desire is to help others understand God's faithfulness to me in the midst of my deepest need.

Finally, it is with deep gratitude that I thank my friends—those in the world of baseball and out—who have been so supportive of me over the years and especially the loving people of Phoenixville and West Chester, Pennsylvania.

Contents

1

The Nightmare

It was the worst imaginable nightmare. In the midst of total darkness I was searching for those most precious to me. Sharp, tiny pellets of snow and freezing rain stung my face. Wind whipped through me like a saber. I struggled to maintain my footing on icy pavement. I was enveloped in darkness, and the only sound was the wind, howling as if someone had turned on the sound track to a horror movie.

Within this seeming void I groped, searching for a vehicle, my van, where my family was trapped. I sensed it without seeing it. I reached out to touch the cold metal and felt my fingertips stick momentarily to the ice-encrusted fenders. Ignoring the numbing pain in my fingers, I clung to the metal, sliding my hands along to the rear door. I slid my hand to where the latch should have been, but it wasn't there. For a moment I shivered, not from the cold but from fear, knowing that my wife and children were inside and I couldn't reach them. Then for an instant the headlights of a car passing on the other side of the turnpike silhouetted the van and I realized that it was lying on its roof, upside down. Then I was in darkness again.

My mind began to revolve as if the dream were fading, only to be revived by two bright headlights pulling up behind me. The nightmare became more disjointed. I was aware of someone by my side, helping me enter the van. We were clawing through a jumbled mass of pillows, seat padding, cupboards, and suitcases. Frantically we searched till we found Andy, my son, buried beneath the suitcases. Back outside, I could see that he was alive and apparently not too badly hurt. He said nothing, but stared at me. This was his nightmare too.

Again my mind seemed confused. If only I could wake up in my bed and feel my wife sleeping next to me. But every time my mind cleared, I was still on that turnpike. Now there were more vehicles around, with blue and red and orange flashing lights that reflected off the icy pavement and revealed snow that seemed not to fall but to fly parallel to the road. "Come this way," a voice said. But I couldn't go. My wife, Gertrude, and my daughter, Theresa, were still trapped inside. "Everything will be all right," they said. "Just get in the ambulance."

Why did they say everything would be all right? "Where is my wife and daughter?" I cried, and this time I heard my own voice. "I have to find them."

"We'll take care of them." It was a police officer. He guided me gently away from the van. He acted like he might know something but wasn't telling me. Why wouldn't he tell me where my loved ones were? He was leading Andy and me toward an ambulance. But I didn't need an ambulance. I was fine. I had to find Gert and Theresa. "I'm all right. Help me look for my wife and daughter."

"We'll take care of them. Now lie down on the stretcher." Again I felt my mind going blank. Hoping that this would facilitate the end of the nightmare, I obeyed. Andy was likewise placed on a stretcher, but all along he stared at me, and without a word communicated, "Daddy, I'm scared." He too was wondering where his mother and sister were. What had happened? Were they all right? As the doors slammed shut and we felt motion in the ambulance, the dream faded into total blackness.

•

My eyes opened to a bright light shining from a saucerlike dish that looked like a radio antenna or perhaps a laser. Certainly the dream was over—a sordid nightmare that would be forgotten in a few hours. But it wasn't; only the scene had changed. On either side I was surrounded by walls of yellow tile. Then above me, out of my line of sight, I heard a woman's voice, asking me to sit up and urinate into a bottle.

Disjointed snapshots quickly flooded my brain. We were driving. Wind and snow were buffeting our van. Then we were out of control. Skidding. There was a scream. The sound of smashing metal. Then silence.

"My wife and children; are they okay?"

The nurse informed me that my son was in the cubicle next door. "But what about my wife and daughter?"

"We don't know yet," she answered. "We'll let you know as soon as we know." My body reeled in a momentary wave of nausea. If I hadn't been lying down, I might have fainted. Again I seemed to fade into and out of consciousness. I was only vaguely aware when I was wheeled into an X-ray room, then back into the three-sided cubicle inside the emergency room. There were images of other tests performed, and questions being asked, and bandages being applied.

Where were my loved ones? My wife? My daughter? My mind demanded an answer. If only I could see them, touch them, hear their voices. I asked again: "Nurse, please tell me where my wife and daughter are."

"We still have no word," she said. For a moment I was aware of two nurses in my alcove, and one was standing over me, cleaning and bandaging a cut above my eye. But I didn't feel physical pain. I couldn't tell if I was seriously injured or not. All I felt was an ache in my stomach, a growing knot that told me something was desperately wrong. Why weren't they in the emergency room? Could they have been sent to another hospital? Or were they so seriously hurt that they were in the operating room? Or in intensive care? or worse....

The nurses finished bandaging my eye and left me alone for a moment. My mind writhed at the thought of two loved ones so seriously hurt but I was not able to help them. I heard the nurse return. "You can sit up now, Mr. Thornton, if you wish."

I sat up on the edge of the cart and listened as she reported that the X-rays and lab tests seemed to indicate no serious internal or head injuries. She also reported that Andy checked out fine. My mind seemed to clear for a moment and began to grapple with the fact that this was reality. "How is my wife?" I asked. And though I hardly dared utter those next words, I was forced to add, "Was she killed?"

"Yes," came the reply, and the nurse started to weep. "Both your wife and your daughter are with the coroner now."

That growing knot in my stomach felt as if someone had crushed it with one of my black- stained baseball bats. My mind recoiled from the impact of that news and my breath momentarily seemed to cease. All that was within me wanted to scream and cry in agony. But my eyes and mouth were unable to respond. I just sat there, numb.

Where does a man go when those whom he knows best and loves most are forever gone? Without any preliminary warning I experienced a devastating loss, as if a limb had been suddenly and cruelly amputated from my body. And then just as suddenly there was a drive to possess the only loved one who was still alive. Though I couldn't remember verbalizing the thought—perhaps the nurses read my mind—Andy was wheeled into my cubicle. Our carts nearly touched, and Andy, while lying down, kept his eyes wide open and fixed on me.

Now, like a homing device, my mind began to slowly and consciously turn. Reality was repelling the tempting, almost-hopeful thoughts that this was a nightmare. Unable to react on my own, my mind and spirit seemed to know instinctively where to turn.

"Would you please bring me a Bible?" I asked. "And would you also call a pastor?" The nurses left, and as Andy and I were together in silence, I became aware of the overwhelming need to pray. Years spent nurturing and developing a relationship with God now took hold automatically. It was like an athlete who, after years of training and practice, finds himself in the most pressure-packed situation, instinctively performing all his skills. Without having to ask, I knew there was only one place to go. There was only One Person who could give me the hope and peace I so desperately needed. As yet there were no words to my prayer, but I was praying. I was simply acknowledging that He was the source of strength I would need to survive the next few minutes. I couldn't even comprehend how to survive the coming days and weeks. I would be content if I could make it for the next five minutes.

I felt my son's eyes staring at me. When he was wheeled in, he was trembling in fright, but now he seemed more calm, though he had said nothing. Silently he slipped off his bed and sat next to me. I held him close and said, "It's just you and me now." I had to tell him the news, but he was only four years old and I wondered if he could comprehend. "Your mother and sister are gone." The thought entered my mind that I never wanted to be separated from my boy again.

Without invitation, flashbacks started to flood my

mind. Rapidly I recalled happy, joyous moments when Gert was so full of life and energy. She had laughed easily and often. We were like two little children full of life and eager to discover everything together. We had delighted in each other for seven wonderful years. She had been my stabilizer, the one who stood by me during a six-year saga through the minor leagues, reassuring me that I could make it to the major leagues, exhorting me to not give up but to reach my true potential. The fact that I had made it to the major leagues was as much a tribute to her perseverance and faith in me as it was to any ability I had.

Then tears started to flow. The pent-up emotions could no longer be contained, and I cried. I thought of Gert as a mother. She was diligent and hard-working, never resenting the fact that she stayed home with the children. She seemed to relish her role, as if it were her calling in life. Any uncertainty came not from dissatisfaction with her role as a wife and mother but rather from a desire, an enthusiasm, to be used by God in a significant way. She believed that she had something to contribute to this world and was eager to learn what it might be.

But her devotion as a wife was total. I recalled how she met me when I returned from road trips that lasted a week or two at a time. She was always at the airport or the stadium to welcome me home. Sometimes it would be 3:00 in the morning and the kids were bundled up, asleep in the back of the car. Now she would never welcome me home again.

My thoughts were interrupted by the nurse, who asked me to come out and speak with the police and coroner. There were questions to be asked, details to cover. Without thinking, without consciously comprehending what I said, I gave the officers the information they needed. When I returned to the cubicle, a man with a red bush beard was waiting. He was the chaplain-on-call, roused in the early morning to come and help.

Again that need to pray swelled within me. Normally a pastor would be expected to pray for the bereaved, but my emotions and thoughts required me to pray. We held hands and bowed heads, and for the first time my prayers began to crystallize into words. They were not words of sadness or remorse. They were words of thanksgiving, thanks to God for the blessings He had poured out on us. There were thanks for the seven years He allowed Gert and me to be together, thanks for the three years little Theresa had been part of our lives, and thanks that they were now with Him. There were thanksgivings for the fact that Andy and I were alive and that God had left us on earth for a purpose. As I prayed, I felt a peace pour over me like a divine bubble of protection coming down and enveloping me. It was a feeling that God was not going to let anyone or anything hurt me at this time when I was in such agony. The pain within was still there, but the nightmare was over. We continued to pray, and I asked God that somehow He would use this tragedy for His purpose. I couldn't comprehend how, but there was a feeling surging within me that God could and would use this loss in a manner that would bring Him great honor and glory.

My mind didn't shut out reality. I was aware that my son, sitting next to me, needed a mother. I could feel the raw sore—not physically, but within—where part of me had been ripped away, never to be returned. I couldn't answer the awful questions. I couldn't answer why. I couldn't even verbalize my needs. But I consciously placed myself in His hands, knowing that He loved me. Other people might question the object of my faith, but I had no choice. If I couldn't turn to Him in this hour of hurt, then I had no reason to live for another moment. The peace

I experienced reminded me that He was real, and that there was reason to live.

How could God heal the hurt? How could He put the pieces of my life back together? How could He make good come out of tragedy? I didn't know the answers. But I knew God. And in this moment I felt myself within the bubble of His love as He was saying to me, "Rest. Be still. Don't move. Just wait on Me."

Within another hour, relatives were informed and hospital forms were filled out. The young pastor volunteered to drive us the rest of the way to West Chester, outside Philadelphia. Only a few hours earlier we had been driving in great joy and anticipation to participate in the wedding of Gert's sister. Now a funeral would replace the wedding. But as we walked out the hospital door that morning, the gloom and fear of the previous nightmare was gone. The bright morning sun had replaced the storm. There was only a hint of chill in the breeze that four hours earlier had brought death-causing ice. It was as if nature had played a cruel joke and was now pretending that it never happened.

But it was real, and I was prepared to face that reality. A few hours earlier, we had been four. Now we were two. God in His sovereignty had allowed two of His loved ones to be removed instantly, without any suffering. Two others were alive and physically unharmed. Though clouded in shock, I was still able to know that God in His sovereignty had a plan for our lives. In the coming months, I would see that plan beautifully unfold.

2

Fear of Death

The confines of the tiny room seemed to press me into my cot. It was late afternoon, and basic training at Fort Dix was in a short recess. Most of the men in my barracks were either on leave or relaxing at the recreation center, leaving me alone in my small room to the side of the dorm. Only the rain, tapping gently against the window, broke the quiet. The cold, gray clouds outside, combined with the dark, army-green walls, accurately reflected my loneliness and depression. Though I had never been in prison, I felt that this was a reasonable facsimile. For the first time in my life I was not my own boss. I was being ordered where to go and what to do. These hours were some of the precious few I could call my own.

Never a gregarious, outgoing person, there were few people I could call close friends, and none of them knew what really concerned me. At least externally, most people would have considered me reasonably content. Only a few months before I had signed my first professional baseball contract with the Philadelphia Phillies, played 19 games with their rookie team in Huron, South Dakota, then spent a few more weeks in the Florida Instructional League. I had some money in the bank and the opportunity to try to work my way up to the major leagues. I was confident, perhaps even cocky, that with my ability and a lot of diligent, hard work, I would have the opportunity to play major league baseball. But that future potential did nothing to relieve my present feelings of melancholy.

I was nearing the midpoint of a four-month stay at Fort Dix, New Jersey. Since I was eligible for the draft and a possible trip to Vietnam, the Phillies asked me, and other rookies like me, to enlist in the Pennsylvania National Guard. First was eight weeks of basic training, then eight more weeks of specialized training. After that I would be required to report for two weeks for each of the next six years, plus be available for duty during any emergencies. This four-month training marked my first extended time away from home, and forced me to come face-to-face with reality.

As I participated in basic training, it was obvious that some of us didn't take it as seriously as others. Some men knew they were headed for combat. I knew I was training to go home in a few weeks. For some men it was a matter of life and death. For me it was like auditing a college class. I was learning the same things and I enjoyed the challenge of doing the best I could in the drills, yet I knew I wasn't going to be tested—hopefully—in real combat. Those who were training to go to Vietnam knew that some of them would return home in a casket, if they returned home at all. Others would return home maimed and mutilated. And for what purpose, I wondered.

Soon after we arrived I was promoted to platoon guide, and while that didn't give me any significant rank, it did mean that I was in charge of a few other privates when a sergeant wasn't available, and that I had a private room instead of having to sleep in the dorm. Now, alone in that room, my only positive feeling was some gratefulness that I wouldn't have to deal with any other people for a few hours.

Being so alone, perhaps it should have helped me to know that my family was only an hour's drive away. But, like so many moments in recent weeks, I felt as if the people I loved the most were on the other side of the world. Though I was permitted to leave the grounds, I had no desire to drive home. I thought about my family background. I was born in Tuskegee, Alabama, at the famous institute located in that area. My father was an excellent baseball player, who could play almost any position and run and hit with power. But because of a growing family he never had the chance to play professionally. He was in his prime before the racial barrier had been broken in the major leagues, and one didn't earn much money in the Negro leagues. So dad worked at the air base in Tuskegee and competed on several semipro teams. My mother went into labor with me on a day that Dad had a game scheduled. He asked Mom to wait until after the game, then he drove her to the hospital with barely enough time to spare.

Dad had grown up on a Georgia farm as one of 13 children. After he married my mother, they moved across the border into Alabama, where they lived for 13 years. I was the fifth of five children born there. I never knew the oldest, Harold. He died at the age of 10, the victim of hydrocephalus, better known as water on the brain. I was only one year old when he died, and we rarely talked about it. But I felt that his loss affected the family more than any of us were consciously aware.

That was what bothered me; boot camp had brought it to my consciousness. Death was something young people never talked about, rarely even thought about—especially a young, healthy athlete like I was. Supposedly I was strong and carefree. But though I didn't talk about it, death was often on my mind. I had few memories of Tuskegee, but one that stood out was a day when I was riding on the handlebars of a bicycle in front of my two sisters, Marietta and Gwen. Our bike hit a bump and threw the two girls into a tree, shaking them up pretty good. Because of my position and the speed we were going, I should have been hurt the worst. But I suffered hardly a scratch. Later my sisters laughed about my good fortune, for I had several close calls but had come through unharmed. "I ducked" was the nickname they gave me.

But I wasn't so lucky a few years later, after we moved to Phoenixville. This city of 25,000 people, located only four miles from Valley Forge, Pennsylvania, was my home for 13 years. Our family had split for a few months, though I was too young to understand why. Mom had taken me with her to Chicago and my two sisters had lived with an aunt while my brother, Billy, remained with Dad. We had been reunited after Dad secured a job in a Phoenixville rug factory and asked the family to join him. I was six years old at the time.

Our home was a 13-room, three-story duplex, located on the wrong side of the steel mill that ran down the middle of town. For a boy, however, it seemed an ideal place to grow up. Only 35 yards from my front door ran the tracks of the Reading Railroad. On the other side of the tracks was a sharp drop to a canal, and just 100 yards beyond that flowed the Schuylkill River. It was a great area to play for young boys with vivid imaginations.

One day while throwing stones from the train tracks I slipped and fell onto two cement culverts that deposited water into the canal. My right arm was seriously damaged, and the doctor had to place pins in it to repair the break. At the hospital they administered some ether, and as I went under I was afraid I would never come back, and I didn't know where I was going. Of course I did return, and the only outward signs of the accident were a few scars on my arm. No one saw the scars, caused by fear, inside my soul.

My best friend in Phoenixville was a boy named

Marshall Burton, who was two years older than I. Since I was big for my age, it was not unusual for me to hang around older boys. We often swam in the river, and during the summer we would trek upstream to the dam. A green sign nailed to the trunk of a young oak tree read "Swimming and Hunting Prohibited," but it hardly interfered with our playing at the river. All of us kids knew it was a dangerous spot, but all of us played there anyway. An old retaining wall behind the tree made an excellent spot for diving into a deep pool of water. From the wall, stretched across the more than 100-yard width of the river, was a dam, and the river poured over the gently sloped cement facing.

One bright summer day three of us decided that it would be fun to slide down the dam into the river. Marshall went first, and another friend, Johnny Sutton, and I followed. Toward the center of the river was a particularly dangerous area, and as we slid down we landed in that spot and were immediately trapped in a circular current and sucked underwater. Marshall came out of the area without problem, but we didn't know that when he hit the river bottom he pushed out away from the dangerous current. Johnny and I were trapped as the whirlpool sucked us down, then we battled back up, reaching the surface for a breath of air before being sucked back down again. Vaguely I could hear friends yelling down the river for help. But help was too far away.

Finally, after what seemed like an eternity, the current tossed us up and away from the suction, and we floated down the river, totally exhausted. Marshall and a couple of men pulled us to the side and laid us on the bank of the river. For two hours I lay there regaining my breath and recovering some strength. My mother would never find out about this, I determined. She had often told us to never go swimming by the dam, which each year seemed to claim at least one life. But what worried me even more than my mother's wrath was the thought, "What if I had drowned? Where would I be now?" One thing was certain—I now knew for sure that there was a God. We should have drowned, but we didn't, and I silently thanked God for saving our lives.

I thought about all the things Marshall and I and other friends had done together. As kids we had played baseball, basketball, and pool. As we grew older we would hang around the street corners together, or steal fruit off some fruit trees, or smash windows in a vacant building. We would party together, and, in order to be part of the group, I would smoke cigarettes or occasionally drink a little beer. We often played cards and gambled whatever little money we had from paper routes or other odd jobs.

One day, hanging around a street corner, one buddy dared me to smack the next guy who came down the street. "How much?" I asked. For one dollar I belted the next kid who walked by us and pocketed the dollar. As we got older, we met some sisters from Reading, about an hour's drive from Phoenixville, and several of us would visit them over an evening or weekend. Finally Marshall married one of the girls, and by the time he graduated from high school we were going separate directions and no longer such close friends.

I would never forget that awful evening when I returned home from playing a legion all-star baseball game. I was walking toward my house on Railroad Street at about 10:00 P.M. Many people were still sitting in front of their homes, chatting quietly with their neighbors. It was a sultry night and the sweat was clinging to my body, trapped beneath my uniform. A neighbor boy came running up to me, yelling, "Have you heard the news? Marshall's been killed!" I was stunned as I heard the sketchy details of how he was stabbed during an argument and had bled to death before help could arrive. Now Marshall was dead. Nothing that I or anyone else thought or did could do anything to change that fact.

As I relived that awful moment, my mind recalled other incidents, perhaps not so vivid, yet just as real. There was Phil, one of my grade school playmates. He was only 14 years old when he drowned in the Schuylkill River. I had been there when the firemen fished out his body, which had turned a pale blue. One man had been shot to death and another injured in a street fight just a few houses down our block. Another man was killed by a freight train while walking on the railroad tracks. A classmate died from some strange disease only a few weeks after her high school graduation. Another close friend, Dawford, was accidentally shot to death on a roller skating rink.

It all added up to a frightening picture for an 18-year-old young man. These were people I knew. Some had been my age, and now they were dead. I couldn't understand why my friends had to die. Where were they right now? In what was called heaven? Or hell? Or did they even exist anymore? And if so, what did they look like? Did they remain the same age? And what about my prospects? Underneath my confidence about life was a fear about my own death. What was the point of it? Why did I have to die? I had no doubt that I could succeed in life. But even if I were tremendously successful and made it to the major leagues and lived in a large home and had a lot of money, that didn't seem like much when I thought about death.

Lying on a table next to my bed was a Bible and a few small tracts that my mother had given me. These were reminders of the many times she had encouraged me to follow Christ. I thought of the time when I played in a biddy basketball program, and our Phoenixville all-star team went all the way to the national championships and I was named all-American. I returned home flushed with pride at my achievement. When the Phoenixville paper came out, I eagerly read the story about our team in the sports section. As I looked through it, though, I became discouraged. Near the end of the story was one little line, "Andre Thornton was also named all-American." That was all. I was crushed, because I thought I certainly deserved more recognition than that, and so I told my mother about it. I never forgot her answer: that I should not worry about awards. If I did my best, God would take care of everything. My performance shouldn't depend on the recognition I received. After that, awards were no longer so very important to me.

My mother and father frequently talked like that to me and my brothers and sisters. These were during the days of racial turmoil in the United States. My dad often told us that there wasn't anything we couldn't do if we worked hard enough, whether it was in athletics or anything else. But being black, there were some situations that created extra tension. I was kicked out of school once because a white girl liked me. The principal had called in her parents and she had lied. This was primarily a white school, and I felt they had wrongly taken her word against mine. Later there was a fight with a white teammate on the football team, and the mayor of Phoenixville had called us and our parents down to his office for a stern lecture. But even though the standards seemed different, Dad and Mom reminded us often that we were not inferior to anyone. Their attitude gave me confidence that I could accomplish anything if I set my mind to it.

There were quite a few Black Muslims in our neighborhood who offered a very logical alternative to the frustration and hostility we felt. But I knew that didn't meet the need in my life. One way of venting my anger was through sports. By the time I was a senior in high school, there was virtually no joy in playing games. I competed with a brutal hostility. Football was my best sport, and I played with the intention of stepping on anybody who got in my way. I took out my vengeance—against whites, against injustice, against the world—on the football field.

After high school, as I prepared to leave home, I think my mother sensed my inner hostility. She was concerned that I didn't follow in the Christian life she so desperately wanted me to have. She would often point out the things I did wrong and tell me I shouldn't do something because "that's a sin." Just before I left for Fort Dix, I had had enough of that talk, and when my mother began to preach to me again, I turned and angrily told her, "Mom, all you ever tell me is that I'm sinning. Everything I do is sin, sin, sin." I had rarely demonstrated anger to Mom before, and as I reflected on that in the loneliness of that barracks room, I knew I had been wrong. I picked up a small red tract. It was a simple outline of what it meant to be a true Christian. Most of it consisted simply of direct quotations out of the King James Bible. Some of them were verses I recognized from my mom's frequent use of Scripture, or from my infrequent church visits. But I didn't put the tract down because the verses seemed to have a new impact on me.

"The thief cometh not but for to steal and to kill and to destroy; I am come that they might have life, and that they might have it more abundantly."[1] Jesus Christ was the Speaker, and He was telling me that He wanted me to experience an abundant life. It was obvious that I wasn't experiencing that life.

The tract continued to quote Christ: "For God so loved the world that He gave His only begotten Son, that whosoever believeth in Him should not perish, but have everlasting life."[2] John the Baptist was also quoted: "He that believeth on the Son hath everlasting life, and he that believeth not the Son shall not see life but the wrath of God abideth on him."[3]

Again I read the words of Christ: "Verily, verily, I say unto you, he that heareth my word and believeth on Him that sent me hath everlasting life, and shall not come into condemnation, but is passed from death unto life."[4] It began to dawn on me that here was the answer to my questions about death. If I believed in Jesus Christ, that He was God's Son, I would experience eternal life in heaven after my death. I had always believed in God and had prayed to Him, though without any confidence that He heard me. Now I was starting to see why. Not only was this the answer to my questions about death, but it was also the key to my enjoyment of life. I continued to read and was surprised to find myself not reacting in anger at the words I saw: "For all have sinned, and come short of the glory of God."[5] And, "For the wages of sin is death; but the gift of God is eternal life through Jesus Christ our Lord."[6] The tract explained that the reason for death is sin. And sin means that men have gone their own way, in disobedience to God. I found myself agreeing with that explanation. It made sense. If God was holy and perfect, why should He allow Andre Thornton into His kingdom? I knew myself well enough to know that I wasn't worthy of the kingdom of heaven. Even if my actions weren't that bad, I knew the evil thoughts I had, and I knew they couldn't be pleasing to God. The reason for injustice in the world was sin. But I couldn't blame other people for my own sin problem.

Now I began to read about the solution. The key was Jesus Christ, who lived a sinless life, then voluntarily gave up His life as He died on the cross. Then, three days later, to prove He was God, He rose again from the dead. I read these verses by the Apostle Paul: "For I delivered unto you first of all that which I also received, how that Christ died for our sins according to the Scriptures; and that He was buried, and that He rose again the third day according to the Scriptures; and that he was seen of Cephas, then of the twelve; after that He was seen of above five hundred brethren at once."[7]

Then the tract got down to the application. Again it quoted Scripture: "And this is the record, that God hath given to us eternal life, and this life is in His Son. He that hath the Son hath life; and he that hath not the Son of God hath not life. These things have I written unto you that believe on the name of the Son of God, that ye may know that ye have eternal life, and that ye may believe on the name of the Son of God."[8] There followed a prayer that the reader could pray, and a place to sign your name, indicating that on this day—and there followed a blank space to fill in—the reader had accepted Jesus Christ as his personal Savior. As I considered what I had just read—that here were clear answers to my questions about life and death—waves of doubt welled up within me. How could I believe this? Was this for real? It sounded good, but could I really trust it and believe it? And if so, what was the evidence?

My mind turned again to my mother. She had always been a very quiet, almost shy woman, steeped in the Southern tradition in which a woman was supposed to stay in the background. She had never completed high school, so she was constantly trying to learn things, and often when she did her housework she would turn on the TV and listen to talk shows where they interviewed experts in various areas.

After we moved to Phoenixville three more children were born into the family. I had been the last of the first wave born in Alabama, but after an eight-year break we quickly grew into a family of seven children. There was a 16-year gap between Bill, my oldest brother, and Greg, my youngest. That put a lot of pressure on Mom.

But what was even harder was living with my father. Dad was a good man, a very moral person. He was a loyal friend, and he taught us early why we shouldn't lie or steal, and that we had to earn our way in the world and stand up for what was right. Unfortunately, he had one flaw that made life very difficult for our family: he had a drinking problem. When he was drinking, my father became a different person. It hurt us all to see the man we loved being destroyed by this devastating, addicting habit.

I had observed how my mother struggled to hold the family together when many times she wanted to leave the situation. Her own parents had separated soon after she was born, and I think that made her more determined not to fail. The problem was that she couldn't endure the fear and uncertainty in her own home.

One morning the television set didn't work, so she turned on the radio. As she began her housework the radio was tuned to a program featuring a preacher named A.U. Michalson on the National Jewish Hour. My mother had always been a religious person, but this particular morning she heard something that made her stop working and listen closely. "Without the shedding of blood," said Michalson, quoting from Hebrews 9:22, "there is no remission of sin."

The preacher went on to explain the purpose of Old Testament sacrifices in which the Israelites offered up sheep, goats, bulls, and even birds. Each animal sacrificed had to be without any flaw, and each symbolized in some way the payment that needed to be made for each person's sin. The sacrifices were symbols of the perfect sacrifice that would be made by Jesus Christ.

For the first time, my mother understood the meaning of the crucifixion. She had heard of Jesus Christ all her life. She had attended church and been baptized as a child. But she had never understood why Christ had to die, and how He had paid the penalty for her sin. Now she truly understood what it meant to be a believer in Jesus Christ.

That happened when I was 11 years old, and my mother was a changed woman after that. She began listening to Christian radio programs every day, particularly Oliver Green and J. Vernon McGee, both of whom systematically taught the Bible. The more Mom studied the Scriptures, the less she seemed depressed by her circumstances. In fact, the joy she felt couldn't be contained, and she told everyone about it. It was obvious as I looked back and examined her life that she now had the peace that allowed her to cope with life, even though her circumstances hadn't changed. She loved to quote this verse, spoken by Christ: "Peace I leave with you; my peace I give unto you; not as the world giveth, give I unto you. Let not your heart be troubled, neither let it be afraid."[9] That peace was obvious in my mother. The reality of Jesus Christ and of His Word were clearly demonstrated in her life.

It was dark now. I had been lying on my cot, reading and thinking for several hours. The uncertainty I had was gone. It seemed that all the loneliness and frustration and depression I had felt today and in recent weeks had led me to this point. God was showing me how hopeless my life was apart from Him, in contrast to the great hope for all eternity that lay in Jesus Christ, if I would only accept Him. I slipped off my bed and onto my knees. "Lord Jesus, I know I am a sinner," I prayed. "Please forgive me of my sins. Thank you for dying for me, and for coming back to life three days later. Please take my life and do what You want with it. Help me not to be afraid of death."

In the back of that tract I cemented my decision, adding my name in the paragraph that read: "I, *Andre Thornton,* accept Jesus Christ as my personal Lord and Savior. He has forgiven me for my sins, washed me through His blood, and raised me up through the living and resurrected Christ." Then I signed my name, and for the first time I felt the assurance that I would never need to fear death again.

Scripture References

1. John 10:10.
2. John 3:16.
3. John 3:36.
4. John 5:24.
5. Romans 3:23.
6. Romans 6:23.
7. I Corinthians 15:3-6.
8. I John 5:11-13.
9. John 14:27.

3

Young and in Love

It was her smile that captured me. It radiated not just from her mouth but throughout her countenance. Her deep brown eyes and heart-shaped face, her delicate facial muscles and fragile cheekbones all joined into a smile that seemed like a celebration of life. Her name was Gertrude Theresa Thomas. Everyone called her Gert.

Amy Williams, the mother of a high school friend of mine, was the matchmaker. I had just completed my first full season of pro ball and taken a job doing ad paste-ups for the Phoenixville daily paper. Amy worked at Wyeth Laboratories with Gert, and introduced us when I went out there to get an ad approved.

Our first date was a few days later—dinner on a Friday night at a small steak shop. As we talked, we discovered that our paths had often crossed. She had graduated from West Chester High, Phoenixville's archrival. Some of her classmates were my toughest competitors in football and basketball. One West Chester athlete, Jon Matlack, had also gone into professional baseball. Gert had made her own mark in athletics, competing for her school in basketball, field hockey, softball, track, and gymnastics.

Right away it was obvious that there was much to attract us to each other. Yet we were cautious. I informed her that I wasn't looking to get married right away; I just wanted to date. She said she wasn't interested in marriage either. After all, she was only 20. I was 21, I told her. It was a lie; actually

I was a year younger than she was. But I wasn't about to risk losing this woman just because she was a few months older. I figured I could explain later if things worked out.

Gert became my first real girl friend. I had dated occasionally in high school, but never seriously. I was a normal teenager who went out and fooled around and did a little necking. But there was never a girl for whom I had felt any sort of love, no one I wanted to date steadily, much less consider marrying. After high school I spent four months at Fort Dix with the National Guard, and most of the rest of my time was devoted to my baseball career. Gert was the first woman I really cared about.

One thing that amazed me about Gert was her energy. She was petite, only 5 feet 3 inches tall and barely more than 100 pounds. Yet her energy level seemed disproportionate to her size. She walked with short, quick steps and all her mannerisms were punctuated by quick, nimble actions. Her speech was also rapid-paced, so that you had to listen carefully to catch each word. Even her laugh, though frequent and spontaneous, came in spry bursts. All these traits reflected a seemingly limitless inner energy. Whatever she did, she did wholeheartedly and enthusiastically.

Much of that was a reflection on her family. All the Thomases—mom, dad, and all five children, of which Gert was second—were hard workers. The parents managed to earn enough to buy a nice home on an acre four miles outside West Chester. Gert's father, Chick, worked for the highway department, and was responsible for road maintenance in the borough of West Goshen. He was very popular in the area, and Gert inherited his outgoing, giving personality. Gert's mom, Hazel, worked for Wyeth Laboratories. She was more cautious and businesslike until she got to know you, but there wasn't anything she wouldn't do for her family. However, someone outside the family, like I was, had to earn her respect. I appreciated her, because she was like I was in some respects, more guarded and cautious of people.

It was the little things that Gert did, when she probably didn't even know I was looking, that told me so much about her. I spent many winter evenings in the Thomas home and observed how after dinner, if no one volunteered to do the dishes, Gert simply got up and did them without complaining or insisting that it was someone else's turn. Her older sister, Yvonne, was married and had a son. Gert and her sisters were always willing to babysit for Yvonne, but I saw Gert change the boy's diapers even when her sister was around and could have done it. It was those little things that added to her beauty and made me see what a special person she really was.

She truly was a beautiful woman. That's something glibly said about many women, yet it was especially true of Gert because her beauty went far beyond the physical. Because of her character and spirit, her attractiveness never faded, no matter how she was dressed, or the condition of her hair, or how much makeup she had on. In my mind, she was always a "ten."

But with her beauty and love and dedication she was also vulnerable. Because she gave so much, she left herself open to hurt. Her love was deep, but her hurt was also deep. I saw it not so much in crisis situations, for that was when she seemed to shine, but at times when some insensitive person would imply that she was not important or valuable. Once, when shopping during the Christmas season, she gave a department store clerk a 50-dollar bill to pay for her purchases. The young woman, perhaps 19 or 20 years old, said she would have to check the bill to make sure it was legitimate. She was gone 20 minutes before returning to say it was all right. Gert was furious. She had worked hard to earn her money and didn't appreciate someone implying that she might be dishonest. It hurt even further to see that for a white customer, a 50-dollar bill was accepted without question.

The confirmation that Gert was the woman for me was her response to my family. I had never brought a girl to my home before, partly out of embarrassment and partly because I had never had a girl friend who was so special. I wondered how, coming from an upper-middle-class background, Gert would react to my poorer, more turbulent environment. I wondered if she could accept my street background and my father, with his drinking problem. But she looked beyond those exterior things and saw the real people. She appeared unaffected by material differences. The smile and openness that captured me also won my family, and she fit in quickly, almost as if she had grown up with us.

The more we were together, the more we realized that we needed each other. We started to seriously contemplate marriage. My primary concern shifted from questions about her to whether she could feel comfortable entering into my baseball life. We had dated for more than a year, interrupted by my third pro season, this one in Spartanburg, South Carolina. My fourth season was with still another Class A club in Newport News, Virginia. It was close enough so that Gert could drive down to see me periodically. I was glad for that because this was a year that made me wonder if I was wasting my time in baseball and if perhaps I should go back to college and pursue a career in teaching or coaching.

It wasn't so much the conditions that bothered me. I could accept the long bus rides, second-rate motels, old ball parks with poor lighting, low salary, and too many meals in fast-food restaurants. It was the uncertainty that bothered me, the fact that so much of your future was determined by other people. I had signed with the Phillies after a spectacular tryout at old Connie Mack Stadium in Philadelphia. Few scouts had taken me seriously when I played high school and legion ball. I was a long shot at best. But in less than 30 swings against pitching coach Larry Shepherd I had belted 17 or 18 home runs, including a couple clear out of the park. That was enough to convince owner Ruly Carpenter to offer me a contract. Though I didn't have the raw ability of some of the other prospects in the organization (future stars like Mike Schmidt, Greg Luzinski, Larry Hisle, and Larry Bowa), with proper coaching and experience I felt I had a chance.

In high school I had played shortstop, but the Phillies moved me to third base. Then there was a setback when I injured my throwing arm at Fort Dix. I never did have a great arm, and the injury made me a liability at third, leaving the Phils uncertain about where to play me. Their solution was to try me at first base. I felt comfortable there, but needed playing time to learn all the intricacies of the position.

At Newport News, the team had a 35-year-old veteran first baseman at the tail end of his career. Most A players are youngsters 18 to 22 years old who are working their way up. We were there to gain experience, to learn the game. We wanted to win, of course, but experience was more important. Our manager, however, had visions of managing someday in the big leagues, and he decided to play the 35-year-old veteran ahead of me, hoping to win a few extra games in the process.

When Gert came down for a week to get a firsthand view of life in the minor leagues, she found me in a frustrated mood. I wondered if the powers in Philadelphia knew I existed, and if I would have my chance to prove what I could do on the field. I seriously wondered if the time had come to leave the game. What made things harder was the loneliness. The only other black player on the team was married, and I had no other friends among my teammates. My roommates were the assistant coach and the trainer, Fred McNeil.

Fred was a veteran of many years in the minors. Actually, he was much more than a trainer. He handled the laundry, swept the clubhouse, packed and unpacked the equipment, and served as traveling secretary. He was a very hard worker. Though never formally trained as a trainer, over the years he observed and learned the necessary skills to do an excellent job. He was a special man who took a personal interest in me. He sat Gert and me down and talked to us like a father. He told us that all ball players had to learn to put up with the system. "Stick it out," he said. "Give yourself a full chance. Don't cut yourself short just because things aren't going well right now." He was a Christian man and he helped me take my focus off myself and realistically look at the situation, and reminded me to allow the Lord to work out the circumstances. It was the type of exhortation I needed at that time.

Gert again proved her devotion. She was not disturbed by my living conditions, or by the fact that I might never rise to the top. She was committed to me, whether I played baseball or taught school or worked in the steel mill. Soon after her visit, Gert and I set our wedding date for October 24. About a month before the end of the season I finally got the chance to play, but I had hardly warmed up when the season was over.

Those few weeks from the end of the season to our wedding day were exciting. Gert was working while I went to school and also worked. One day she sent me a little note with five dollars in it because she

Gert and I on our wedding day, October 24, 1970.

had heard I was low on money. It was a small gesture that reconfirmed how much we really loved each other. It told me how committed she was, that everything she had was dedicated to helping me succeed. In turn, it motivated me to want to give all I had to her.

Our wedding was an exciting day for us and our families. But because of our jobs and my school, we didn't take a honeymoon. That didn't seem to matter, for we were young and in love. We didn't have much money, but someday, when we had saved and had the time, we determined we would have our honeymoon.

Our love seemed to grow even faster after our marriage. We occupied a brand-new, comfortable one-bedroom apartment. Since Gert worked during the day and I worked swing shift, our schedules made it difficult to have enough time together. But we stole every minute we could, especially welcoming a couple of snowy days when it was easy to convince ourselves that we were snowed in.

Of course we had normal adjustments as a couple, things that all newlyweds go through to one degree or another. When two separate lives, with two sets of habits and patterns of living, are merged into one, each side has to adjust. But our little disagreements were so insignificant that time soon erased them from our memories. We were two young people who were very much in love and eager to face life together.

It was our faith that provided the vital foundation for our marriage. Gert grew up attending church and had made her commitment to Jesus Christ at a young age. Hers was a simple faith, yet alive and vital. It was a faith that took God at His Word; she believed God and acted accordingly. My footing was more uncertain. I was like a baby learning to crawl and then to walk. I would stand up, wobble a bit, perhaps take a step, then fall right back down. But I kept at it, and gradually I was able to take a few steps at a time.

The evidence of my spiritual growth wasn't obvious at first, but I noticed certain attitudes gradually change. My language was the first. At the time I was in Fort Dix, almost every other word was a swear word. After my conversion I prayed about that. "Lord, I don't want to curse," I said. On my own I couldn't stop, but He took it away. Then I noticed my desire for cigarettes dwindle. It wasn't an instant decision to quit, but a gradual realization that I was going longer and longer between smokes, until I didn't want to do it anymore. There were other areas where God convicted me. I had learned a lot in the streets. While growing up I didn't see things like sex outside marriage as wrong, but rather an accepted part of life. Soon after my conversion, God started convicting me about these attitudes, showing me where I was wrong, and He started to reconstruct my thought processes. In short, He was beginning to transform my life.

At first my mother was my main source of spiritual growth. The times when I was home were special because she would give me books to read or would discuss what she was learning from the Bible. I had lots of questions, and she seemed able to answer them all with great wisdom. Many times we would sit together and listen to a Bible teacher on the radio. Dr. J. Vernon McGee was my favorite. He was an elderly preacher from Texas with a distinctive Southern twang. His doctors told him that he was dying from cancer, yet God seemed to keep him alive year after year, postponing the inevitable so he could teach the Word of God. All he did was teach the Bible, book by book, chapter by chapter, verse by verse. His program, "Through the Bible," took us through the entire Bible in 2½ years, and then again in a five-year period. When he finished, he started another five-year cycle. It was Dr. McGee's basic, easy-to-understand teaching that gave me my early knowledge of Scripture.

Gert was just as eager to learn, and she would bring her Bible when we visited my mother. She would join us as we listened to Dr. McGee, or enter into my discussions with Mom. It made me proud to see Gert, who was well-educated, eagerly sit and listen to my mother, who hadn't completed high school. Gert could see that my mother was wise not because of her worldly knowledge, but from more than ten years of diligent study of the Scriptures.

Unfortunately, my spiritual growth often slowed during baseball season. Away from the influence of my mother, it was easy to slide—to not read the Bible or listen to the radio programs. That was one way Gert helped me after we were married. As I would pack my bags for a road trip, she would remind me to pack my Bible and would encourage me to pray and read the Word each day when I was away from home. Sometimes when we were separated we would talk on the phone and end our conversation in prayer. She was the constant encouragement I needed to grow and mature toward becoming the man God wanted me to be.

We had an added blessing that first year of our marriage when I finally advanced to the Philadelphia AA club based in Reading, just an hour's drive from West Chester. In order to save money, we moved into Gert's parents' house, and Gert would drive to Reading after work and watch me play. Then on road trips she would drive me over in the morning before leaving for work and pick me up when the team returned, a few days later. It was not unusual for us to arrive back home at 3 A.M. after a night game, but Gert never missed meeting me.

Our first year in Reading turned out to be the break

I needed professionally. For the first time I participated in more than 100 games. I had my highest batting average as a pro, hit 26 home runs, and led the team in runs-batted-in. After that season the Phillies invited me again to their instructional league program for six weeks in Florida, where we celebrated our first wedding anniversary. For us that was almost like a honeymoon as for six weeks we worked out and played our ball games during the day and then were free each evening.

The next year we started the season in Eugene, Oregon, with the Phils' AAA team. I opened the year on the bench, but when the starting first baseman got off to a slow start I replaced him and played well. After 46 games I was hitting better than .300 for the first time in my career and was leading the club with 29 RBIs. One of the benefits of playing in the Pacific Coast League is that Hawaii is part of the league. We decided that Gert would make that road trip with me, giving us almost a second honeymoon.

The morning we were to leave for Hawaii, the phone rang. I glanced at my watch and noted that it was only 5 A.M., the midnight hour for baseball players who play mostly night games. I lifted the receiver and heard my manager, Andy Seminick, on the line. "Andre, I've got some news for you," he said. "You've been traded to the Braves."

Immediately I was wide awake. For several years I had hoped and prayed for an opprotunity to play in another organization. The Phillies seemed loaded with talented first basemen, and I didn't want to be a player who spent his career mired in the minor leagues. If the Phillies didn't see me in the major leagues, I wanted to go to an organization that did. Moving to the Atlanta organization, even though it was with their AAA team, meant a new beginning for me.

But with this trade, and the new opportunities of

fered, came a lot of practical headaches. The floor of our bedroom was strewn with open suitcases in preparation for our trip to Hawaii. Now there would be no trip to Hawaii, but our packing job was halfway completed. While the team would be leaving for Portland and the flight to Honolulu in a few hours, we had to inform the apartment manager that we were vacating our apartment, hoping that someone else would pick up the lease. We had to make our own travel arrangements to Portland, book flights to Richmond, find a new apartment in a strange town, and report to the new club, all within a period of about 48 hours.

It was in situations like this that I saw how strong Gert was. This is the side of professional baseball that most fans never see. It's something that is particularly difficult for wives. Men can usually adapt quickly to a change, but for the wife, her security is in her home and the relationships she has with her friends in the community or with fellow wives on the team. In one moment those relationships can be severed, and for many women a few moves like that are extremely traumatic.

But Gert never complained. Her attitude was that we were in this profession together and that she would do whatever was necessary. In only a few hours we packed, left the apartment, and boarded a flight for Richmond. With the Braves my average didn't remain at the lofty levels I had achieved in the Pacific Coast League, but in just 49 games I ended up tying the team for the lead in home runs. But an even bigger thrill was when we learned that Gert was pregnant with our first child.

Andre Thornton, Jr.—little Andy—was born in December. He arrived six weeks earlier than expected, so when Gert went into labor we thought she was just sick. We finally went to the hospital, and Andy was born 30 minutes after Gert was admitted.

He weighed only four pounds, and because he was premature he stayed a few extra days in the hospital before coming home.

Gert and Andy stayed home while I went to spring training with the Braves. A few days before the season opener, the Braves broke camp and headed north with Henry Aaron as the starting first baseman and Andre Thornton as backup. On our way north we played several exhibition games. Three days before the regular season was due to open, I injured my leg while breaking up a double play at second base. Since the injury would sideline me for at least a week, the Braves decided to send me back to Richmond.

That was a tremendous disappointment, and things didn't get much better when I dislocated my shoulder and ended up missing another month. Then, soon after Gert and Andy joined me in Richmond and we had settled into an apartment, I was traded again, this time to the Chicago Cubs via their AAA team in Wichita.

Again we packed up and moved, but I wondered if this would be any better situation than what I had left in Atlanta. In Wichita I went on a hitting spree, belting 17 home runs in 40 games, and the call came from the Cubs to report to the major leagues. Nearly seven years and eight different teams after I had entered professional baseball, I had reached the pinnacle.

I don't believe it was coincidence that my rise to the big leagues began with our marriage. I'm convinced that without Gert I would never have made it. She was the stabilizing influence I needed. She was the one who calmed me when I got upset with the management. She was the one who soothed me when some insensitive oaf made a wisecrack from the stands. During the times when I debated whether to remain in professional ball, she encouraged me to stick it out, to finish what I had started, and to let God decide the outcome. It wasn't that she longed for life in the major league lights. She wasn't motivated by material things. Even after we made it to the majors, she was never frivolous with money. She had an old coat that symbolized her attitude. It was warm and comfortable, though several years old, yet she felt no need to buy a new one as long as the old still did the job. I knew Gert would be content anywhere, as long as we were together. She wanted me to be happy. But she knew me well enough to know that I had to continue on until I reached the top or else the final door was shut in our effort. The fact that we succeeded was as much a testimony to her dedication as it was to my ability.

4

Laying the Foundation

It was one of those rare days that is perfect in every way, when the normal worries of the world are squeezed out by the joy of being alive. It was a day when I was especially conscious of the blessings of a wonderful wife and two beautiful children, plus many friends and family, an exciting career, and a purpose for living. Perhaps in all our lives there are only a handful of such days in which the joy is so great that we feel we can't take any more happiness.

It was a time for optimism—a new beginning. In a couple of days I would be leaving for spring training with a new team, the Cleveland Indians. The struggles of the previous season, with an abysmal .191 batting average, had faded like a bad dream.

This particular Sunday I loaded the family into a new Dodge van outside our West Chester, Pennsylvania, apartment house. The weather was cool, crisp, and clear on this February morning. After buckling Andy and Theresa in their seats, Gert slid into her seat next to me for a short drive to church. Normally we attended Bethel A.M.E., a small church located just a few blocks from downtown West Chester. But today we passed Bethel and rounded the corner for St. Luke's. Like Bethel, it was a simple two-story stucco building with a brick front. On this day I was scheduled to be the main speaker for a special youth day service.

The city of West Chester, with a population of about 30,000, was like a second home to me; it was located just 14 miles from Phoenixville, where I had spent 15 years growing up. I enjoyed the recognition that goes with being an excellent athlete in the area. Each year I would return home to the warmth of special friendships, and the daily paper would update my progress for a growing local following.

When Gert and I married, in 1970, West Chester became our home, first in Gert's parents' house and then later in our own apartment. When in 1973 and '74 we finally reached our dream of the major leagues, our achievement was in part the achievement of two small towns in Chester County, west of Philadelphia. And with that recognition came invitations to speak and share, especially in churches like St. Luke's, since people had heard about and witnessed many changes in our lives.

These speaking opportunities were special, and, as was my custom, I worked hard to prepare a message. Rather than tickle the audience with stories about my baseball career, I tried to leave them with something substantial, something that would demonstrate that there was more to Andre Thornton than just professional baseball. I didn't want people to leave the building thinking, "What a great person Andre Thornton is," but rather, "What a great God Andre Thornton has!"

After a brief introduction by the pastor, I entered the pulpit and looked over some 200 people jammed into the main sanctuary and small balcony. The light from a single, stained-glass window above the balcony, along with similar windows along the sides, overpowered the church lights. I opened my Bible and read from the second chapter of Ephesians:

> But God, who is rich in mercy, for His great love with which He loved us, even when we were dead in sins, hath made us alive together with Christ (by grace ye are saved), and hath raised us up together, and made us sit together in heavenly places in Christ Jesus, that in the

ages to come He might show the exceeding
riches of His grace in His kindness toward us
through Christ Jesus. (Ephesians 2:4-7).

As I read, tears began to well up in my eyes and
I felt again the incredible power of this passage by
the Apostle Paul. I paused for a moment before
starting my message. It wasn't like me to lose my
composure in front of an audience.

"The Lord has done so much for me," I said, and
briefly recounted how God had made Himself real
in an army barracks in 1968, and how He had taken
me and my wife through a growth process while we
spent six years in the minor leagues. I told how the
previous winter, while playing baseball in the
Dominican Republic, God had moved us to totally
dedicate our lives to His service, wherever that
would take us and whatever would be required.

To graphically demonstrate just how powerful and
rich God's mercy and love is, I told a story. It was
about a man named Horatio Spafford who lived in
Chicago in the mid-1880s. He was a successful
lawyer and real estate investor, and also a committed Christian who served God alongside his close
friend, evangelist Dwight L. Moody. Along with
Moody he helped start a daily noontime prayer
meeting that helped bring spiritual revival to Chicago
and launched Moody into an international
evangelistic ministry. Then in 1871 all of Spafford's
business and investment holdings were destroyed in
the great Chicago fire. Only because he lived out in
the country were his home and family spared.

Over the next two years this man, with his wife,
Anna, and their four daughters, worked hard to
restore their lives from the devastating setback. In
November of 1873 they planned a trip to Europe. A
last-minute business opportunity prevented Horatio
from departing with his wife and daughters, but he

promised to catch up with them in France within a few weeks. Anna and the four girls set sail aboard the S.S. Ville du Havre from New York City.

However, halfway across the Atlantic their ship collided with an English steamer and sank in just 12 minutes. A total of 226 people perished in what was one of the worst sea tragedies ever. Anna was among the 57 survivors, but all four girls were lost. When she arrived in Wales, Anna wired her husband with these words: "Saved Alone."

For some reason I couldn't understand, this story tugged at me emotionally. I could feel my throat tighten as I related how Mr. Spafford sailed for France to meet his wife, and as he passed over the location where the Ville du Havre had gone down, he started writing a hymn that has become a powerful encouragement to thousands of Christians. As I looked at my notes I could barely focus because of the tears that were now flowing involuntarily:

> When peace like a river attendeth my way,
> When sorrows like sea billows roll,
> Whatever my lot, Thou has taught me to say,
> "It is well, it is well with my soul."
> Though Satan should buffet, though trials should come,
> Let this blest assurance control:
> That Christ has regarded my helpless estate,
> And hath shed his own blood for my soul.
> My sin—oh, the bliss of this glorious thought—
> My sin, not in part but the whole,
> Is nailed to the cross and I bear it no more;
> Praise the Lord, praise the Lord, O my soul!
> And, Lord, haste the day when the faith shall be sight,
> The clouds be rolled back as a scroll;
> The trump shall resound and the Lord shall descend;
> Even so—it is well with my soul.

Why should I be so emotional about this particular story? The church was absolutely still; even the youth who might be excused for squirming sat quiet. I backed away and tried to regain my composure. It was hard to understand, much less explain my emotions. I wasn't sad. On the contrary, I seemed to be filled to overflowing with the Spirit of God. Yet I wondered if my spirit was trying to tell me something. I couldn't tell. All I could say in conclusion was that God had been so good to me, and the mercy and grace He had demonstrated to Horatio Spafford in the midst of such a tragedy was available to me and to everyone in this building.

As I ended my talk, my emotions stabilized and I introduced Gert to the congregation. She in turn introduced her parents and sisters. "Praise the Lord," she said. "I want to say that I'm very proud of my husband, and thankful to the Lord for him. I'm also thankful that the Lord has come into our home and into our hearts." For the second time that morning, I was choked up. This was the first time I could remember Gert getting up and saying anything before such a large group of people.

After the service many people came forward to greet us and thank us for what we had shared. It seemed that many were affected. There was one person in the audience to whom God was particularly speaking. Her name was Pat Vallot, the wife of my second cousin, Al. They lived downstairs in the apartment directly below us. She went home and spent the rest of that day and evening reflecting on our God and the things we had told her in church and during the previous months. Finally she reached a conclusion and called us about 3:00 in the next morning. Gert answered. "Gert, this is Pat. There's nothing wrong, but can I speak to Andre for just a minute?"

I took the phone, "Andre, guess what? I'm saved!"
Pat's husband, Al, had been tragically paralyzed in
a car accident nearly a year before, and we had tried
to help them during their period of crisis and adjustment. But they had a difficult time understanding
how God could allow such a tragedy. Pat had struggled with a new baby and a full-time job, plus caring for an invalid husband. She had despaired even
to the point of considering suicide. All Gert and I
could do was be there, to listen, to encourage, and
to try to point them to the hope that we had in Jesus
Christ. Now Pat was telling me that she had found
the answer. She was experiencing personally the inner peace that we had told her about. As we hung
up, my gratitude to God was overwhelming. I
couldn't imagine feeling any more happiness or joy.
If only this day, this moment, could be savored the
rest of our lives. I might accomplish more thrills in
baseball, maybe even participate on a championship
team. But there was nothing to compare with the joy
of helping someone you love experience the ultimate
reason for living.

In retrospect, because of events that would occur
later, this day stands out in my mind. Perhaps it sym-
bolizes how far God had brought Gert and me. In
1970 we were toddlers in faith. Now we were like
adolescents, eager to step out and prove our love for
God. We were willing to go anywhere, do anything—even die, if need be, to bring glory to Him.

Surprisingly, it was my success in baseball that led
to this point of commitment. In many respects, the
fulfillment of my major league dream was a letdown.
In 1975 I suffered a broken wrist and missed two
months, yet came back to lead the team in home
runs. Just a few more at bats would have ranked me
fifth in the National League for slugging percentage.

I was an unknown who in his first two seasons
compiled a respectable record. So I was surprised

how little joy I derived from it. For one thing, there wasn't much camaraderie on the team. Everyone did his job, but beyond that the players went their separate ways. It seemed so empty, so meaningless. It wasn't the satisfying experience I thought it should have been.

Most of my happiness came at home. I never tired of spending time with Gert and our children. Theresa was born in March when I was in Scottsdale, Arizona, for spring training. Shortly after that I broke my wrist, so I went home to see the baby and helped Gert drive the family to Chicago.

Both of our children brought us great joy. Andy and Theresa were totally different personalities. Andy was a little like I am: shy, slow to warm up to strangers, yet very giving and open when he got to know someone. Theresa was the family ham. When I would come home, Andy would hang back, but my little daughter would come rushing into my arms. She was full of life and energy, and loved to entertain us. These were two special children, each with a unique personality, each special in his and her own way.

Gert was extremely effective as a mother. She could handle just about anything in the home as well as or better than I could. And what she couldn't handle, someone in her family could. She was never afraid to do whatever was necessary to get a job done, which gave me confidence when I was away from home.

Once during the off-season, while I was working out at the gym, Andy fell against the corner of our apartment building and split his lip. Gert was seven months pregnant at the time, but without considering her condition or trying to find transportation, she picked up our son and ran a quarter of a mile to the hospital, where the emergency room staff gave him four stitches. Another time, shortly after Theresa was

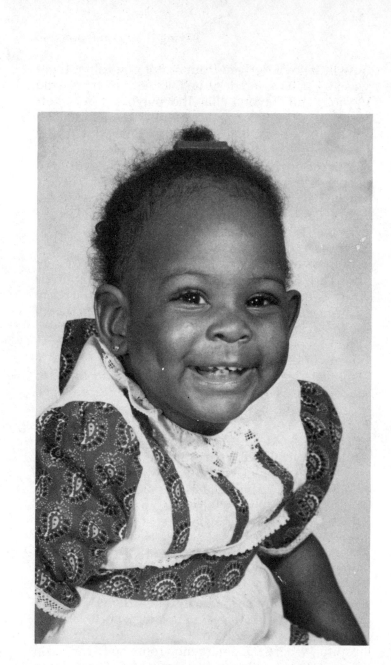

My daughter Theresa.

born, Andy decided to jump into a swimming pool, though he had no idea how to swim. Gert, without removing any clothing, immediately jumped in and pulled him to safety. When Theresa was a little older, Gert began teaching both of the children how to swim.

When I made the Chicago Cubs team, we were finally able to stabilize our family routine. For half the year we lived in Chicago while I played with the Cubs. The rest of the year we occupied our second-floor apartment in West Chester. It wasn't the best arrangement, but at least we weren't moving several times a year to different cities scattered around the country.

Following my successful 1975 season, I received an offer to play winter ball in the Dominican Republic. Gert and I decided to take advantage of this opportunity to earn some extra money in the off-season, so instead of moving back to Pennsylvania, the whole family went to Latin America. That winter was a crucial time for us spiritually. It seemed that we were ready to advance into deeper waters. We no longer were content to just be successful in sports. We no longer were content to be simply known as Christians. We no longer were content to be like spiritual children, drinking milk from the Word. We wanted more. We needed meat in our spiritual diet. We wanted to serve God in a substantial way.

Part of our spiritual longing may have been due to the conditions we found in the Dominican. Here we were, successful ball players from the United States, placed in the midst of incredible poverty. We watched several kids scavenge for food in garbage cans behind our apartment, and finally invited them over and fed them. It was an eye-opener to see the poverty, and to realize that overflowing grocery store shelves didn't exist in this country. Many people went to bed hungry at night.

While the poverty sobered us, there was more. In the Dominican Republic, there was a lot of time to study the Word. As I studied, I couldn't help but feel an uneasiness within that told me God wasn't first. God demanded total dedication to Him, ahead of everything else. I could see that baseball wasn't satisfying me. A big house wouldn't satisfy me. Money wouldn't satisfy me. Even my family, happy as we were, wouldn't ultimately satisfy me, because people inevitably let us down. My only fulfillment would come from a total commitment to the Lord.

The Cubs had been one of the first major league teams to hold chapel services on Sunday, and now most teams were doing the same. Quite a few ball players were coming to Christ. But it takes time to grow, and I was impatient. I saw in them and in me a desire to grow, yet many weren't spending time in the Bible and seeing their lives become conformed to the standard that God sets in His Word. It was so easy to let the everyday business of baseball keep us from doing what was most important.

Independently, Gert was having similar thoughts, and we began to discuss them. We would read the Scriptures together and lie in bed late at night discussing the need to allow God to have total reign in our lives. One day we received a letter telling us of my cousin Al's tragic automobile accident and the news that he would probably be a quadriplegic the rest of his life. Gert and I talked about what it would be like if that happened to me. Would my life be ruined because I could no longer play baseball? If my commitment to the Lord was total, I would know that He was in control of my life and that there wasn't anything that couldn't turn out for good with the Lord.

During this time Gert was studying the book of Job. This man had been incredibly wealthy, but God allowed him to lose everything except his wife and his own life. All his property was destroyed, his seven children were killed, and his body was covered with painful boils. Gert observed how Job's friends were unable to help him because they didn't know God. We wondered why Job, a godly man, had to suffer so greatly and the wicked didn't. What was the purpose of this test? Job's friends gave him plenty of advice, but it was futile; it didn't soothe his misery. Only when God spoke at the end of the book was there an answer.

In Job 38 and 39, we read how God answered Job with a long series of questions: "Where were you when I laid the foundation of the earth? Tell Me, if you have understanding, who set its measurements, since you know? Or who stretched the line on it? On what were its bases sunk? Or who laid its cornerstone?...Have you ever in your life commanded the morning, and caused the dawn to know its place?...Where is the way to the dwelling of light? And darkness, where is its place?...Can you lead forth a constellation in its season?...Can you lift up your voice to the clouds, so that an abundance of water may cover you?...Can you hunt the prey for the lion, or satisfy the appetite of the young lions?...Do you know the time the mountain goats give birth? Do you observe the calving of the deer?...Do you give the horse its might? Do you clothe his neck with a mane?...Is it by your understanding that the hawk soars, stretching his wings toward the south? Is it at your command that the eagle mounts up, and makes his nest on high?" (NASB).

Finally God challenged Job: "Will the faultfinder contend with the Almighty? Let him who reproves God answer it." Job could only answer, "Behold, I am insignificant; what can I reply to Thee?" (NASB). Like Job, when I saw God as He really is, I realized my insignificance. I saw my sinfulness and my unworthiness. But God didn't stop there with Job or with me. When Job admitted his total dependence on God, God restored all that he had before, and more. God was ready to do that for me spiritually, for He said through His Word: "Blessed be the God and Father of our Lord Jesus Christ, who has blessed us with every spiritual blessing in the heavenly places in Christ" (Ephesians 1:3 NASB).

Gert and I lay in bed one night talking about these facts. We could both see that the greatest joy in life came through knowing God, through obeying Him and being used by Him. We wanted to be used by God. Here in the Dominican Republic we saw great poverty. But even worse, we saw people with no hope. All across the United States we saw people in the same spiritual condition. They had every material need, but they didn't have any reason for living. We wanted to help them. And to help, we had to be faithful to the Lord. We wanted a deeper love for Him. We wanted to respond to His conviction quickly and allow Him to clean up our thoughts and habits and inner desires. It was as if God was telling us, "Get ready, because I am going to use you."

That night we prayed together and asked God to take our lives totally and completely. I no longer wanted to be known as a baseball player who happened to be a Christian athlete. Gert didn't want to be just a baseball player's wife, or a mother. We wanted to be a man and woman of God. We wanted to serve Him, whatever that meant, whatever that required. We wanted Him to use baseball as a vehicle for spreading His name.

When we returned home, we tried to minister to my cousin Al and his wife, Pat. We arranged for them to secure the apartment below us. Both of them were going through traumatic adjustments. Al was having to learn how to live all over again, knowing that he could never walk and do the things that most people find routine. Pat was pregnant with their first child and having to adjust to a husband whom she would have to care for the rest of her life. Both had great needs, and we tried to help meet some of them. I would spend hours with Al, reading the Bible to him and giving him books to read and Christian records to listen to. Pat came by the apartment to talk, or she would stop me in the parking lot on the way to and from my workouts. Gert and I loved them, prayed for them, and pointed them to the hope we had in Christ.

This time period was a high point for us spiritually. We had committed our lives to the Lord and He started to use us. But then God saw fit to take us through a valley. Though not afflicted like Job, I experienced frustration on the baseball field. I got off to a slow start in 1976, and then the Cubs traded me to Montreal for pitcher Steve Renko and outfielder Larry Bittner. We gave up our apartment in Chicago, and Gert went home to West Chester and saw me only on weekends when we played in Montreal. I found the Canadian city difficult to adjust to. I didn't like the cold, and I felt out of place in the French culture. On the field I struggled. I broke one finger and jammed another and was never able to raise my batting average above .200 for the season.

But in the midst of such struggle we often receive great blessing. In the Bible, it seemed that God often drew His leaders into the desert for a time of teaching and growth before using them for ministry. It happened to Joseph, Moses, David, Elijah, and the Apostle Paul. I felt I was in a type of desert, yet in the midst of my struggles professionally I was finding the Bible coming to life. I was having long periods of time to study and read and listen to tapes. I was learning and growing in a manner I never thought possible, and as a result I was experiencing a peace in the midst of the difficult season, a peace I would not have experienced just a couple of years earlier.

In Montreal, God brought a man into the clubhouse one day who became one of my closest friends. Dave Fisher owned a Bible book store in Peterborough and had a ministry of writing letters to players. We immediately began to share, and he began giving me books that he thought might be helpful. We would fellowship in the clubhouse or over the phone, and he would send me letters of encouragement.

God was using my faith as a witness to my teammates and other people around me. One day I was interviewed by a reporter who later told me he couldn't believe an athlete could have that kind of peace in the midst of such a difficult season. The evidence of God at work in my life helped him make a commitment to Christ.

Probably the key lesson I learned was an understanding of the Person and work of the Holy Spirit. Since I had never studied this, one day I picked up a tape series on the subject. I did not want to restrict the work of the Holy Spirit in my life, for Christ had taught that the Spirit would teach us all we needed to know, and would direct our lives. That's what I wanted—God through His Holy Spirit to actually control every detail of my life. Only then could I be sure I was pleasing Him. The key was faith—believing that what Christ said was true, and acting on it. Rather than attempting to make myself a better person, I began to allow the Holy Spirit to implement what I had learned through the Word.

After that season in Montreal, Gert and I were invited by the Fellowship of Christian Athletes to participate in a Bible study with the Philadelphia Eagles during our off-season. Each week we met with players like John Niland, Randy Logan, Charlie Smith, and Harold Carmichael, and their wives. This was another important step for us because it provided needed interaction and fellowship with other Christians in professional sports. Baseball, like football, had chapel programs on Sunday for each team, but few baseball teams had any other form of fellowship. Many of the football teams were having midweek Bible studies that helped couples delve into the Scriptures.

Gert and I would often discuss those lessons. She had many valuable insights, but was hesitant to share those thoughts with the group. Most of the wives were younger than Gert, and I felt she had a lot to offer these women. One night, as we prepared to go to the study, Gert went back to our bedroom just as we were ready to leave. When I checked on her, she was on her knees praying. In the car I asked her why she prayed. She explained that she knew she had a lot to contribute to the study, but was afraid to share. She was praying that God would give her boldness to open up and share her thoughts with the rest of us. That night she did open up, and that was the beginning of a greater boldness to share her faith.

That same off-season we attended a conference by Pro Athletes Outreach in Florida. There nearly 100 pros, primarily from the National Football League, gathered to learn from outstanding teachers about the Christian life, including areas such as family, finances, and how to effectively share their faith. Gert returned from that week eager to put those principles into practice.

Then we learned that I had been traded to Cleveland, and we felt we were being given a new beginning. God had taken us through the valley, and there He had laid a foundation for us to begin an effective ministry. We decided to make our home in Cleveland and settle down as a family. There we would be available to minister to teammates and their wives. Perhaps we could start a Bible study on the team. We wanted to grow personally, but we also wanted God to use us on the team and in the city. Little did we know just how dramatically God would fulfill those desires.

5

Heading Home

We enjoyed traveling at night. It was a habit we had started when I played for Chicago. There was less traffic at night and we were more relaxed. The children could sleep in the back while Gert and I alternated driving. Sometimes we would listen to music on our tape deck, or perhaps to a Bible lesson; other times we would simply use the quiet time for thinking or resting.

Gert and I were well-organized. Years of switching homes two or three times a year honed our technique. We could pack for an extended trip and be on the road in just a couple of hours, and it took even less time to unload and settle at our destination. We were like a precision team, with each partner instinctively knowing his or her responsibility.

It was a Sunday evening when we loaded our van for a trip to West Chester. Cleveland's baseball season had ended only two weeks before, and the Dodgers were currently playing the Yankees in the World Series. It had been a gorgeous fall afternoon, and all around us the trees were in a symphony of color. Of course, I realized that many of those colorful leaves would have to be raked when we returned from Pennsylvania.

Gert and I were busy cleaning and fixing our new home, the first we had owned in seven years of marriage. It was a spacious ranch-style brick house set on 2½ acres outside Chagrin Falls, a suburb of Cleveland. It was a quiet place near a man-made lake, far from the roar of the stadium crowd and the clamor of the big city.

The projects were numerous. Gert made curtains while I cleaned the basement. There were floors to polish, cabinets to clean, appliances to put in place, shelves and drawers to line, a roof to patch. The list was endless. But it was enjoyable work that we didn't want to leave even for a day. Gert was happier than I had ever seen her. For the first time she had a home, a single place where we could settle down as a family for the entire year. Sure, there would be road trips during the season and six weeks of spring training, but the family no longer had to wonder where home was. And with growing kids, including a son ready to enter school, that was very important.

We had originally planned to spend two weeks back in our hometowns after the season. But that had already been reduced to one week. Gert's youngest sister, Jenny, would be married the following Saturday, and Gert was a bridesmaid. We would return home the following day.

We had started our Sunday with church. During the season I rarely had the opportunity to attend church, so it was good to get back into the Sunday routine where we worshiped together as a family. Back home I began packing the van while Gert fried some chicken for dinner. Our van was customized for comfort on long trips. In the very back, over the luggage compartment, we made up two beds in which Theresa and Andy could sleep, behind the back seat. Between there and the captain's chairs in front were cabinets and a refrigerator. I stacked two suitcases by the window just in front of the back seat.

As we prepared to leave, I checked the weather report. Rain was forecast, meaning an end to the sunny weather we had enjoyed for several days. There was also a chance of snow squalls at higher elevations. I didn't concern myself with that, knowing that it was early for any significant snow accumulation, and that the turnpike was usually kept clear in any case. Then Gert noticed a purse left by a friend who had visited us the previous evening. We decided to drop it by on the way out of town.

It was dark when Andy and Theresa climbed into their beds. Always before starting a long trip I would pray for our journey. If I happened to forget, Gert would remind me. This time she prayed, the first time I could remember her volunteering to do so. "Lord, thank You for this beautiful day," she said. "Please give us a safe journey and bless our time with the family. Please especially bless Jenny as she prepares for her special day. In Christ's name, Amen."

As we backed out of our long driveway, several large raindrops splattered on the windshield. By the time we were on the road into Chagrin Falls, my wipers were clearing away a light but steady rain. As we rounded one sharp curve, I noticed that a car had slid off the road. We pulled over to see if we could help. It was a nurse returning home from work, and she told us that help was on the way. Gert nervously encouraged me to move on, since we were stopped at a dangerous point in the road. So we continued on our way.

After dropping off the purse in Cleveland, I headed onto the turnpike and drove for two hours. As we entered Pennsylvania, Gert took the wheel. She put an Andrae Crouch tape in the tape deck while I leaned back and tried to sleep.

But my mind was actively reliving several exciting moments during the past year. The hum of the engine and the passing road lights seemed to stimulate me to think and meditate. It had been an unusual baseball season. Though primed for a peak performance, the season had started slowly. In fact, the entire team had struggled. Manager Frank Robinson had attempted to shake up the team and had benched me in the process. Then he was fired, and a coach on the team, was named to replace him.

Gert and I had spent many hours in prayer during those days. We knew that God had brought us to Cleveland, and we were excited about what He had in store for us. But it was frustrating to not perform to our full potential on the field. Still, there were rewarding moments. In spring training we were able to start a Bible study on the team, and several players and their wives participated. After the regular season started, there were opportunities to share in Cleveland, especially through the news media.

Gradually my play improved and I started hitting the ball solidly, though the hits still didn't fall at first. Several weeks into the season I had a chance to speak at a church one Sunday evening following an afternoon game. After that talk Gert and I had sat in the living room of our fifth-floor apartment in West Cleveland and reviewed what God had done since our decision in the Dominican Republic. There was the team Bible study that continued during each home stand. I was taking a correspondence Bible course to learn more systematically about the Scriptures. There was the ministry with Al and Pat, and we continued to talk regularly with them on the phone.

We spoke enthusiastically of our future in Cleveland. There were many churches that I could speak in. I had dreams about an outreach during the off-season to the inner city of Cleveland, to distribute Bibles and maybe hold some youth rallies. And I was excited about perhaps buying and operating a Christian bookstore, a business we could continue after pro ball was completed.

Gert shared my enthusiasm for these projects, yet she questioned her role. She spoke quickly in her animated manner. I had to smile as she got excited, because her voice rose in pitch and the words seemed to pour out even faster. "Andre, I can see how God is using you. You're speaking, playing baseball, having articles written about you. But I wonder how the Lord is going to use me?''

Her question surprised me. I quietly assured my wife that God was mightily using her. She was an excellent mother and wife. A man couldn't ask for a more loyal and loving partner. She had supported me through all the years in the minor leagues without ever complaining about our tight budget. And now that we had made the big leagues, there was no impatience on her part to make up for ''lost time'' by rushing to buy a big house or obtaining other material benefits.

Our increase in ministry was also a team effort. True, Gert wasn't a speaker. She didn't have a public image. But she did help greatly with the Bible study. She shared with other wives on the team. And she was tremendously supportive to me in all that I did.

Gert seemed to appreciate what I said, yet there was more to it. She realized that each life has a special purpose. Gert saw that I was finding my particular area of service. And Gert could see the role she was playing. Yet she said again, more slowly this time, ''Still I wonder, how is the Lord going to use me?'' It was said as if she knew that God had something very special for her. He was going to use her in a unique manner, and she was not afraid of what that might be; in fact, she eagerly anticipated it.

That little incident persisted in my mind. I didn't understand what Gert was saying, but I sensed that it was important. What particularly impressed me was her desire to be used. We both felt that way. We wanted our lives to count for all eternity.

I mentally reviewed the rest of the year. Things on the field had improved the second half of the season. On July 8 my batting average was only .184. Then I arrived in a hitting groove, and for more than two months I batted over .350. I finished the season leading the team in home runs with 28, and I tied for the American League lead in fielding percentage among first basemen. It had turned out to be my most productive year professionally.

But I was even more satisfied with the team Bible studies which had continued all season. No longer were Gert and I simply taking in the Word. We were also attempting to give it out. I reflected on the day in Minnesota when I had invited then-coach Jeff Torborg to go with me to a Bible study with the Twins. Minnesota pitcher Geoff Zahn had invited me to join him and some of the other Christians on the team like Jerry Terrell and Tom Johnson. I wasn't playing well at the time, and Jeff asked me to explain how I could be so calm in the midst of such a difficult time. I explained how my life was committed to the Lord, and that if I really loved Him I couldn't just praise Him when things were going well; I had to praise Him at all times. We talked about that, and Jeff shared about the death of his father the previous winter, and how difficult it was for him to understand and accept it. A few weeks later Jeff was named manager. We had a special relationship, closer than I had ever had with any previous manager.

I interrupted my reflections and turned on the CB for a moment to see if there were any problems ahead. I heard scattered reports that the weather was worsening. It didn't sound serious, but I left the radio on low and returned to my meditations.

Gert and I had looked at homes for a couple of months and had had several opportunities to buy. But none of the houses seemed right for us. We prayed that the Lord would show us something in keeping with our lifestyle—something roomy but not ostentatious. We finally looked east of the city. The house we found was perfect for our needs, and an excellent buy. We moved into the house in mid-

August, feeling that God had provided generously.

Toward the end of the season there were two memorable moments for me. Before our last home game of the season, a Sunday, we had a chapel service in which the speaker was a black evangelist named Howard Jones. Howard was an associate evangelist for the Billy Graham association. I enjoyed his teaching from the Word, and we talked after the service. He told me that he lived only a couple of hours away, and would enjoy spending some time together in fellowship. So we exchanged addresses and phone numbers.

My one disappointment in Cleveland was the fact that we didn't have much fellowship apart from the team. The Christian community, though welcoming my public witness for Christ, seemed somewhat standoffish, as if waiting to see what kind of a person I really was. In a way I could understand their cautious attitude. They had seen professional athletes profess Christ, and then turn around and denounce Him by their actions. They wanted to see if I was for real. Still, I longed for closer fellowship, and perhaps Howard Jones would provide that opportunity. I made a mental note to call him when we returned from our trip.

After that Sunday we had taken our final road trip through New York and Toronto. We lost the first three games against the Yankees, but on Thursday afternoon we beat them 4 to 1. It felt good to win, knowing now that they were division champions. That evening, back at the hotel, I pulled out a book to read. I usually carried a couple of books with me on each road trip. *Tested by Fire* was the title, and it was written by Merrill and Virginia Womach. "A True Story of Courage and Faith" read the words across the cover, which featured an impressionistic painting of a man diving away from an exploding airplane. I didn't generally read biographies unless they dealt with some real struggle. Most celebrity biographies seemed shallow; I wanted to read stories that showed how people had worked through difficult problems.

This seemed to be such a book. It was the story of a man who was piloting his single-engine plane homeward on Thanksgiving Day when he crashed in poor weather. He escaped alive, but with third-degree burns over much of his body, including all of his face.

For the next few years he endured dozens of extremely painful operations. For this couple it was a severe test of their faith. For Merrill there was intense, unceasing pain, the uncertainty about his future as a singer and businessman, plus the stigma of a horribly disfigured face. For Virginia the suffering was perhaps even more difficult because she not only had to take care of her husband but also assume responsibilities as both father and mother to their three children.

For some reason this book captivated me. I called Gert that evening and told her about it. We both thought of Al and Pat and how this might minister to them. I continued to read into the early-morning hours, and as I did I seemed to gain a better understanding of the suffering they were going through. I had never had to suffer like Al, or like Merrill Womach. Now I was gaining some insight into the depth of their suffering, but also into the tremendous grace available to people who trusted God in the midst of that suffering.

It was 5 A.M. when I had finally completed the book. We had an 11 A.M. flight to Toronto, so I left a wake-up call order at the front desk and went right to sleep. The next thing I knew it was 11:00 A.M. I had missed my wake-up call, the team bus, and the flight. I didn't even know which airport we were supposed to fly out of.

Fortunately, I guessed right with LaGuardia, and our traveling secretary had made arrangements at the ticket counter, so I made it to Toronto in time. But the usual fine for missing a plane was 500 dollars. That would be an expensive book. When I arrived at the park, manager Jeff Torborg asked for an explanation, so I told him about the book I had read and how I had stayed awake all night reading it. He accepted that and didn't fine me. When I arrived home, Gert read the book too. Rarely had either of us read a book that caught our imaginations in such a strong way. I anticipated giving it to Al and Pat. In fact, we had just talked with them recently, and Al said he had some exciting news for us when we got to West Chester.

"Ready to switch?" Gert's voice brought me back to the present. We were coming up to a gas station, about halfway through our trip. Gert pulled in and we made a quick, routine switch. As I started to pull back onto the turnpike, Theresa stirred, then walked up front and climbed onto Gert's lap. Within minutes, both were asleep.

The CB was still on low, but there was little activity. Only an occasional crackle or hiss broke the silence inside the van. It was about 3:00 A.M. now, and there were few people on the road. The wind had picked up and we were now driving through snow mixed with freezing rain. I slowed down and kept the van at a steady speed of about 40 miles per hour.

We were in the mountain passes of Pennsylvania, and this narrow turnpike seemed like a wind tunnel. Occasionally a gust of wind blasted the side of the van, as if to push it off the highway, and left us vibrating in its wake. I reached the top of a hill where the road straightened into a long, flat stretch. The only light I could see was my headlights boring into driving snow. The wipers quietly swished back and forth at their highest speed. Briefly I noted a green sign indicating that we were approaching Somerset. I pulled over into the passing lane, where the traction seemed firmer. There was no other traffic on the road, so I would play it safe and give myself extra room in this weather.

My senses seemed keenly alert. I was aware of every nuance of the gusting wind, sensitive to any slip of traction. We had driven through difficult weather before, worse than this, and I felt in control of the situation. But it would help if they would sand the road, I thought.

Then another blast of wind rocked the van, and suddenly I was no longer in control. The rear tires slid right, toward the guardrail, pulling the rest of the vehicle with them. I jerked the steering wheel right, trying to break the skid. But the whole van was sliding. I ripped the wheel back and forth, then lightly touched the brake pedal, trying anything to stop the skid. I was aware of a scream—a shrill, terror-filled sound. The van kept sliding, and I was powerless to stop it. The right fender smashed against the guardrail post, reversing the slide, but then my mind went black and I saw and heard no more.

6

Through It All

Looking back on the days following the accident, my memories seem like they're shrouded in fog. Occasionally the haze clears and I'm left with an image. But those moments are disjointed. It's as if someone took a series of snapshots and then scrambled the pictures. Some days remain unaccounted for. My primary memory is that I felt as if God had sealed me off from the world, with only a few necessary individuals allowed to intrude.

I remember only vaguely the four-hour ride from Somerset Hospital to West Chester. Andy slept most of the way in the back seat. I can recall sitting, still in shock, staring out the windshield and saying very little. But the pastor, Wayne Sauter, who drove us says I talked almost the entire trip, reliving the accident, trying to figure where we went wrong, reviewing portions of Gert's and my life together, and voicing hope that God would somehow use this tragedy for great good. But I don't remember talking about these things. Over the following days and weeks my mind would retrace those thoughts many times until certain conclusions crystallized in my mind. But on that trip the intense shock of the previous hours made any conclusions premature.

There was one traumatic moment when the hearst from DeBaptiste Funeral Home in West Chester passed by us on the opposite side of the turnpike. My emotions, somewhat controlled until then, snapped, and I wept, knowing that this vehicle was going to pick up the bodies of my two loved ones.

But after a few minutes those feelings stabilized somewhat and I was aware again of God's calming influence in my life. All I had to do was relax within that presence.

Another heart-rending moment came as we arrived at the Thomas home. How many times I had driven up their long driveway! On my first date I was so nervous that I parked several minutes near the entrance before daring to proceed. But later, as I became one of the family, that driveway meant home and fun times. My mind spontaneously remembered outdoor barbecues that Gert enjoyed so much, as well as birthday parties, Thanksgiving dinners, and New Year's Day gatherings. As Wayne parked, Chick came out to meet me. As I embraced his short, stocky frame, I began to sob. Tenderly he stopped me and urged me to be strong. They were counting on me to set the example and hold things together.

Graciously Chick invited Wayne inside for a cup of coffee. Then after a few minutes Wayne excused himself and headed back home. It's the only time I ever saw Wayne, but I hold a special place in my heart for that pastor. God sent him that day specifically to minister to me. As he left, Wayne volunteered to return to the scene of the accident and search through the van for my billfold, Bible, and other valuables. He promised to ship them back to me in Cleveland.

I can remember people coming by the house during those next few days. But the faces are blurred. I had difficulty distinguishing individuals—there were too many. There were phone calls from around the country, plus cards and telegrams. I was aware that people were concerned and were expressing their love and support and prayers. Someone told me that every major league team had sent condolences. People all over the United States were uplifting me and my family.

One newspaper reporter managed to reach me that first afternoon. Normally I was very cooperative with the press, but this time I couldn't cope with it. "I can't talk now," I told him. I don't remember saying anything else, but I must have done so because the reporter quoted me as saying, "I want to get over the shock. Our faith in God has always been strong, and He will give us strength to handle even this." Mercifully, that was my only encounter with the media that week.

I was acutely aware of the fact that Gert's family had also experienced a great loss. While mindful of my own deep hurt, my heart also ached for them. I wanted to reach out and comfort them as they in turn reached out to me. We pulled together and hurt together as a family. They knew how deeply Gert and I loved each other, and I knew how close Gert had been to each member of the family. I thought of how Gert had come home not too long ago to care for her mother after she had been in the hospital. With all her sisters working, Gert was needed, so she cared for Hazel, baby-sat several nieces and nephews, and prepared the meals. When we were away from West Chester during baseball season, she called once or twice a week and wrote to her family often. That was the type of devotion she had. The joy she brought to Chick and Hazel, to her sisters Yvonne, Joan, and Jenny, and to her brother "Little Chick" would be missed. Who could possibly fill that vacuum?

Everyone hurt deeply, but there were things that needed to be done, numerous details to be taken care of, and the character of that family was to pitch in and help. Chick Thomas acted as my prompter, gently informing me of the next decision that required my attention. We had to visit the funeral home, mortuary, and church, and then plan the funeral service, choose a headstone, and fill out insurance claim forms.

One incident still remains vivid in my mind. Perhaps it was my most difficult moment of the week. I was sitting with the funeral director in his office. We had discussed the caskets and had decided to place Gert and Theresa together in one simple coffin. The director handed me their personal effects and asked me if I wished to keep Gert's wedding ring. "No, I'd like the ring to stay on her finger," I answered. Then I asked if I could see Gert.

"Andre, that won't be possible," he answered. "However, you can have a viewing for Theresa if you wish." The knot in my stomach that kept me company in the emergency room returned. I had seen her for the last time in this life. For a moment, the grief was unbearable. It had all happened too suddenly. If only I might have been warned, if there had been just a little preparation. I needed one more look at the woman I had known and loved for the previous seven years.

Later I could look back and acknowledge that it was best I did not see Gert's body. That way I could remember her as she really was—alive, vibrant, and cheerful. Seeing her once more would not have comforted me, for that was only her physical shell, not the real person I had loved. But at that moment it was almost too much to bear. Thankfully, God's peace was incredibly real, and in His presence the hurt gradually subsided and was pushed toward the back of my mind.

Later people often asked me at what moment I felt God's peace. From that moment on the emergency room bed when I knew Gert and Theresa were dead, I knew God's peace. It wasn't something that was only printed in a Bible verse; it was real. That peace enabled me to remember that we had a God who loved us, and I knew that He would not allow this thing to happen unless He planned it that way. That didn't mean He caused the accident, but that He

knew it would happen. He could have prevented it.
He could have intervened. But He didn't. So I believed He would give me all the strength and help
I needed to endure it. I knew I was trying to live for
the Lord, and therefore I had confidence that He
would not let me down. Even though I could not
begin to comprehend why this happened, I felt His
closeness, and that gave me strength to praise Him
and thank Him. I knew He was there, and I knew
God would not take such a wonderful saint as Gert
without having a tremendous purpose. Gert was a
woman who had lived for the Lord. Therefore I was
confident that she was with Him now. If that belief
was shattered, then my whole basis of life and hope
was shattered. But I could rest on the facts, and in
that I had peace.

All week the Thomas house was constantly full of
people. Relatives, neighbors, friends, church
members—everyone had to come by. There were
many tears shed. People tried to comfort me, but it
was obvious that most of them didn't understand
God's sovereignty. They questioned why God would
take such a dear woman. They questioned the meaning of her death. They questioned why good people
like Gert were taken instead of wicked, evil people.
These people saw my peace and questioned why I
was not distraught.

Several times I sat down with questioners in the
dining room and opened my Bible to explain the hope
I had. I showed them 2 Corinthians 5:8, where Paul
wrote: "We are confident, I say, and willing rather
to be absent from the body, and to be present with
the Lord." Gert knew the Lord. Now that she was
gone from us, we knew she was with Him, and
Theresa too.

I showed them Hebrews 13:5: "I will never leave
you nor forsake you." Those weren't just words on
a printed page; they were reality, and I was experiencing it.

I showed them Revelation 21:1, 4: "And I saw a new heaven and a new earth; for the first heaven and the first earth were passed away, and there was no more sea ... And God shall wipe away all tears from their eyes; and there shall be no more death, nor sorrow, nor crying, neither shall there be any more pain; for the former things are passed away." As Christians, this was our hope. Our suffering was temporary. Someday there would be no more anguish.

I showed them Matthew 10:28, where Christ said, "Fear not them who kill the body, but are not able to kill the soul; but rather fear him who is able to destroy both soul and body in hell." I explained that it wasn't death we should fear. We needed to understand God, and the greater fear—that of eternal separation from Him—if we didn't know His Son.

I showed them John 5:24, where Christ said, "Verily, verily I say unto you, he that heareth my word and believeth on Him that sent me hath everlasting life, and shall not come into judgment, but is passed from death unto life." The issue was what did we do with God's Son. That determined our attitude toward death.

Without consciously realizing it, my healing was beginning not because of what others said to me but because of the power of the written Word of God. I wasn't relying on condolences and emotions and family and tears. I was counting on the Word. My mother was a tremendous encouragement, for she came over several times and ministered to all of the family. She cried with us, but she also gave us hope, and that hope was in Scripture. She pointed over and over to promises that God made in His Word.

The day before the funeral, my mother called me. "Andre, I dreamed last night that I should give you this verse—1 Peter 1:25: "The Word of the Lord endures forever." She said that at first she didn't understand why she should share that particular verse until she read the entire chapter. My mother was practicing this truth, and I began to realize through her encouragement that this would be the key to my healing.

That night I read 1 Peter Chapter 1 slowly and saw the comfort in those verses. "Blessed be the God and Father of our Lord Jesus Christ, who according to His great mercy has caused us to be born again to a living hope through the resurrection of Jesus Christ from the dead, to obtain an inheritance which is imperishable and undefiled and will not fade away, reserved in heaven for you, who are protected by the power of God through faith for a salvation ready to be revealed in the last time. *In this you greatly rejoice, even though now for a little while, if necessary, you have been distressed by various trials,* that the proof of your faith, being more precious than gold which is perishable, even though tested by fire, may be found to result in praise and glory and honor at the revelation of Jesus Christ" (verses 3-7 NASB).

I stopped and mediated about the living hope that we had in Christ. I knew, based on this and other Scriptures, that Gert and Theresa were enjoying the fulfillment of their inheritance. I could rejoice in that and thank God that when my work on this earth was finished, I too would gain the inheritance and would see my loved ones again. I could thank God that He had a special plan for Andy, and, much as he missed little Theresa, he too would see her again someday. Yes, it was evident why Peter told us to rejoice, even though for a while we had to go through fire.

My meditation and Bible reading melded into a time of prayer, and the three continued simultaneously. For a while time seemed suspended as I drew strength from my Lord and from the Scriptures. I thought about that last verse—that the proof of my faith might be found to result in praise and glory and honor at the revelation of Jesus Christ. I prayed that my life would be a testimony for the Lord, even beginning the next morning at the funeral, and that as a result of my faith other people would praise Him.

I read on in the chapter and came to verse 13: "Therefore, gird your minds for action, keep sober in spirit, fix your hope completely on the grace to be brought to you at the revelation of Jesus Christ" (NASB). I reflected that my hope was not the hope of the world. My hope wasn't in wishful thinking. My hope was in the certainty that Jesus Christ would someday return, and until then His grace would be sufficient. I knew I couldn't stand up under this pressure, but I knew His grace would more than compensate for my inadequacy. Just thinking about this hope instilled me with strength. Though sad and tearful on the outside, my spirit was vibrant, almost exultant.

I read on. "If you address as Father the One who impartially judges according to each man's work, conduct yourselves in fear during the time of your stay upon the earth; knowing that you were not redeemed with perishable things like silver or gold from your futile way of life inherited from your forefathers, but with precious blood, as of a lamb unblemished and spotless, the blood of Christ" (verses 17-19 NASB).

I had lost a dear wife and beautiful daughter. But my loss couldn't compare to the suffering that God had endured for me. I thought of Christ's suffering— the way His skin was ripped off His back by the scourge, how He was spit on and mocked, how the thorns were shoved into His head and the nails driven into His hands and feet. I could not deny His love for me. He had paid the price to redeem me from my sins. Much as I hurt, I couldn't doubt His love. My suffering couldn't compare with His.

This led to an exciting climax that concluded with the verse my mother had shared that morning: ''Since you have in obedience to the truth purified your souls for a sincere love of the brethren, fervently love one another from the heart, for you have been born again not of seed which is perishable but imperishable, that is, through the living and abiding word of God. For 'All flesh is like grass, and all its glory like the flower of grass. The grass withers, and the flower falls off, but the word of the Lord abides forever' '' (verses 22-25 NASB).

This tragedy rammed home how temporary life is. Gert had lived 29 years, Theresa two. Like a flower that blooms for a few days, they had lived a few short years. Now they were gone. Was there anything that was permanent in such an unstable world? Yes, the Word of God always remains. It has endured for thousands of years, and will endure long after this earth has passed away.

These words encouraged me greatly as I prayed for Andy, my family, and the Thomas family. I urgently asked God to give them the peace and encouragement He had given me. Then I began to pray for the funeral service, which we had decided to call a Service of Triumph. As I prayed, I felt a compelling desire to share this hope I had. God seemed to be telling me that He wanted me to speak to the congregation, to encourage them to trust Christ before another person in that church building passed away. No one expected me to speak. It wasn't part of the program. It wasn't normal for the bereaved spouse to speak at his loved ones' funeral. But I felt compelled to break tradition and bring hope to those who were crying for hope. Emotionally it would be difficult, but what God required of me He would provide the strength to accomplish. I finished praying, fell into bed exhausted, and slept deeply.

The next morning was clear and cool. I put a

sweater underneath my jacket for extra warmth. The Bethel A.M.E. church was jammed to capacity and many people had to stand outside and listen through the open doors. Cars were parked four abreast, bumper to bumper, even on the sidewalks, so it was difficult to reach the front door. Though I paid little attention to who was in the congregation, I did notice several members of the Cleveland Indians: owner Ted Bonda, manager Jeff Torborg, public relations director Randy Adamack, and teammates Buddy Bell and Duane Kuiper. I appreciated that they had made the effort to come and be with me.

In front, the casket containing the two bodies was practically buried beneath the most flowers I had ever seen in a church. Many were from baseball people around the country. The commissioner plus the National League and American League offices had sent bouquets, as well as individuals such as Frank Robinson, Hank Aaron, and Bill Robinson. All of them were trying to say they cared. My desire to share the hope I had with them increased even more.

The pain of grief was too much for my son. He had been very quiet during the week, and at the service he simply leaned against my side and cried himself quietly to sleep. I knew again that the Lord was protecting us. This little boy couldn't endure any more, and there was nothing I could do to help him right now. God eased his pain by putting him to sleep.

It was an emotional service, opening with the hymn "The Old Rugged Cross." Scriptures were read, Rev. Matthew Jones prayed, and Elizabeth Butler, a family friend, acknowledged the hundreds of cards and telegrams that had already been received.

So far I had managed to maintain my composure. Then the Nicholas Choral Ensemble began to sing this song by Andrae Crouch, and my emotions could no longer be contained. My body sobbed as I listened to the words.

> Through it all,
> through it all,
> I've learned to trust in Jesus,
> I've learned to trust in God;
> through it all,
> through it all,
> I've learned I can depend upon His Word.
> I thank Him for the mountains,
> and I thank Him for the valleys;
> I thank Him for the storms He's brought me
> through;
> for if I never had a problem,
> I'd never know that He could solve them,
> I'd never know what faith in God can do.

Of all the songs, this one surely said it all for me. It expressed my prayer that through this tragedy I could trust in Jesus and his Word, and that God might demonstrate to the world what He could do through me. I thought again of those people sitting in the congregation. Many of them didn't know my Lord. Many of them didn't understand the hope I had. I wept, thinking that many of these people who were close friends could die today and they wouldn't be with Gert and Theresa because they had refused to cling to that old rugged cross.

I had told the pastor that I wanted to speak, but after he finished the eulogy and benediction, he turned to end the service, forgetting my request. So I rose, took little Andy by the hand, tapped the pastor on the shoulder, and he sat down. Together, Andy and I stood in front of the casket and faced the congregation. Tears flowed freely as I started to speak. "There are tears in my eyes, but my heart is comforted," I said. "The reason I'm standing here now is because you knew Gert and Theresa and you know what our lives represented. You know how we tried to live our lives for the Lord. We thank God for giving us a chance to touch as many lives as He made possible.

"Today, these tears you see are not for me. These tears are for you, and I pray that before one of your lives is stolen away, before another person here passes away, each one of you would ask Jesus Christ into your life and would know Him as your Savior."

Then the service was over and we began the procession to the cemetery. At the Rolling Green Memorial Park, with major highways bounding us on two sides, the casket was set down and a short, simple service conducted. Behind us was a large statue of Christ, arms raised toward heaven. Again I reminded myself that my two loved ones were not going down into the earth. They had already departed. But the ache returned, more intense than ever. It seemed so final. I would never again touch them or hear their voices in this world. I would never sit little Theresa on my knee and bounce her while she joyfully chattered to me. I would never again experience those intimate moments with my wife, the times we kidded each other, or sat and talked in a restaurant, or lay in bed and prayed. I would never again be able to phone her while on a road trip and hear her reassuring voice and know how much she loved me. The service was over. The casket lay in the hole, dirt splattered over it. People drifted away quietly until I was alone. Never had I felt so empty. The ache increased. The knot in my stomach grew. I couldn't think about anything except how much I missed them. Never could I love someone as deeply as I had loved my wife. That vacuum could never be filled. Part of my life was down at the bottom of that ditch.

"Andre, are you all right?" It was my mother. It was said as though she wondered if I might climb into the grave. "Yes, Mom, I'm okay." The spell of that moment was snapped, and I turned and headed toward the parking lot. Though I was emptied, I had to go on. As I headed toward the car, I noticed Al and Pat Vallot waiting. They greeted me warmly and told me they had come by the house, but because of Al's wheelchair and the crowd of people inside, they hadn't come in. Al looked up at me and smiled. "Andre, I understand a little of what you're going through." I knew he did. Others had said that, too, but Al really did understand. "I want you to know that I have come to know the Lord! And I know that He can heal your pain." I cried again, though not for sorrow. Al began to encourage me that God could take me through this trial. He was trying, it seemed, to repay the many hours spent ministering to him and Pat. It was as if he was saying, "Let me return some of that love to you."

Gert had played such an important role in their lives. We had ministered to them together as a team. She would have been so happy. Their encouragement was a tremendous spiritual boost, for I knew from this moment that even as Gert had touched this couple's lives, she was going to touch many other lives in the coming days and weeks. Though she had departed, her ministry wasn't finished. In fact it was just beginning. Al and Pat had provided a glimpse of how God was going to use Gert's life in a powerful way.

7

Sowing Tears

The trees surrounding the backyard were like a grandstand slowly emptying after a game. Many of the colorful fall leaves lay on the grass in front of me, but their colors seemed subdued on this cloudy day. A slight breeze blowing off nearby Lake Erie dropped a hint of the coming winter. In just a couple more weeks the trees would be stripped bare, except for a solitary pine tree in the far corner of the triangular lot.

Sitting on a lawn chair in the patio, I felt like those trees—stripped emotionally. The events of the past ten days had served to exhaust me to the degree that I despaired of ever being fulfilled again. The shock of the news and the frenetic pace leading up to the funeral had dissipated, and I was now alone. Gone were all the well-wishers and sympathizers. My family and Gert's family were continuing their jobs and responsibilities. My teammates were home with their families. There was no job to divert me from facing an empty home and an empty heart. And I sat there, staring into that emptying grandstand, and I prayed.

I was alone, yet not alone, for the reality of the Scripture verse "I will never leave you nor forsake you" was explicit. Previously that had been a nice verse to know. People had quoted it to me, and I had shared it with others. But now it wasn't simply a nice platitude: it was reality. I knew that God was with me. I was experiencing Him.

Within His reassuring presence I prayed the most

intense prayer of my life. I was like a little child who comes running to his mother crying, yet he can't explain where it hurts. So he simply points. Mother always seems to understand, and she wraps him in her arms and loves him and then ministers to his hurt.

I could not verbalize the intense agony within me. But I could point and know that God understood. His arms wrapped around me, and as I was enveloped in His safe, protective bosom, I poured out my soul to Him. It was prayer like I had never known, for it contained no words. Rather, my whole body and soul were given to prayer. There were so many things to pray about that I couldn't begin to even touch them, but God understood. The verse where we are taught that the Holy Spirit intercedes for us, was reality. God's Spirit understood totally, and he took over and prayed for me. It seemed like my whole body groaned with Him with an intensity that overloaded my nervous system.

How long I sat there I cannot say, for when my body could no longer stand the trauma, I fell into a deep sleep in the chair. When I awoke, I felt refreshed and strengthened. The agony was relieved. Though my open sore wasn't healed, it was like the child who has been comforted by his mother—it simply didn't hurt quite as much.

For the first few weeks after returning to Cleveland I had many moments like that one. Over and over again the pain would swell and I would go to my heavenly Father and point. Sometimes I would sit in the patio and at other times in the living room or my office. It didn't take much to trigger the hurt. I would see something of Gert's or recall an experience we had shared together. The curtains she was making lay on the sewing table, waiting for her finishing touches. There was an old note she had written to me, lying on my desk. Her study Bible sat open on

the nightstand. A favorite cookbook stood ready for
her dinnertime use. A pile of folded clothes waited
to be put away. The same was true with little
Theresa. I would see one of her toys or a closet full
of her little dresses. Each reminder of their absence
brought quiet tears and led to prayer.

Often Andy was with me. These were precious
moments which the two of us had together. There
were people who had suggested that I send him away
to stay with friends for a few weeks. Some had hinted
that his grandparents should raise him, or that he
be placed in a boarding school. The implication was
that a child this young couldn't cope with grief, and
therefore should be removed from it. These people
meant well by their advice, but I wanted Andy with
me. We needed each other. His loss was just as real
as mine. Removing him from his home wouldn't heal
his hurt. Andy knew that his playmate and friend,
Theresa, would not be coming back. He knew he
would never see his mother again. His pain and grief
were just as intense as mine, and yet the Lord also
had him in a protective bubble. Removing him from
me would not have served his needs.

That didn't mean I knew how to help Andy. I
didn't. But I could pray. Words of agony poured out
toward God for him: "Lord, I can't do a thing for
Andy except give him to You. You have allowed this
to happen and so only You can give direction. Only
You can take this boy and be to him a father and
a mother. I'll do everything I possibly can to guide
and teach him in the love and admonition of the
Lord. I can love him, but only You can heal his
heart." I knew that the Lord understood what
Andy needed, so I wasn't going to compromise and
give in to what the world said he needed.

For a while Andy slept in my room with me, and
many nights he would wake up from nightmares.
The turmoil of the crash, the fear inside the hospital,

the confusion of a little child lost without his mother—these would crowd in on him and he would wake and cry. I would hold him and together we would pray.

It was in little ways that I learned what he was feeling. We had a four-wheel drive truck that gave me trouble. The engine stalled at the most inopportune times for no apparent reason. One snowy night we faced a long drive home when the truck stalled. Andy slammed the dashboard and said emphatically, "Dad, we've got to get rid of this truck." I had never seen him so angry. He said what I, feeling skittish about cars anyway, already felt. We were stranded with no CB and nowhere near an open gas station. So we prayed together, and then turned the key again, and the truck started right up. We drove more than an hour the rest of the way home, and when we finally pulled into the driveway, only then did it stall again.

We often talked about why Mother and Theresa weren't coming back, but that we would see them again someday. Andy turned six on December 10, and during our little party he asked me, "Does Theresa have a birthday in heaven?" I tried to explain that in heaven there probably wasn't any time as we know it. But it was difficult for a little boy, much less a grown man, to understand the concept of eternity.

Then he asked, "Does Theresa stay the same age or does she get older and grow up like I do?" I couldn't answer that question. All I could do was assure him that she was with God and that when we saw her in heaven, I was confident that we would recognize her.

We didn't talk a great deal about the accident. Neither Andy nor I could remember many details. He was asleep when it had occurred, and awoke within a whirlwind of flying debris inside the over-

Ron Kuntz

Our times together were very important to both of us.

turning van. He told me that he was thrown off his bed and that our two soft leather suitcases had fallen on top of him, protecting him from serious injury.

One evening Andy asked me, "Dad, why did we leave at night?" Pangs of guilt gripped me for a moment. It was a question I had asked myself many times. "Well, son, we always traveled at night," I answered. "Why do you ask?"

"You asked that question in the hospital," he told me. I didn't remember, but it was probably true. I asked a lot of questions that night, questions that still plagued me. I gently tucked my son into bed and we read a story together from the picture Bible Gert had bought him. After we prayed I turned out his light and went into the living room and began to weep. Horrible mental pictures flooded my mind as I relived the accident. Apart from Gert's scream, however, it was a silent movie.

Why had we departed when we did? The "What ifs were so convicting. If we had left an hour earlier we would have missed most of the storm. If we had left an hour later the road would have been salted. What if Gert hadn't noticed her friend's purse? We would have been on the turnpike at least 45 minutes sooner. If I had realized how much ice was on the roads, I would have pulled over. But I wasn't aware of that danger. Besides, I had driven in worse conditions.

There were so many questions. If we had slid just ten more feet, Gert and Theresa would still be alive and probably unharmed, for the guardrail post we hit was the last one before a large turnout. We might have spun around in there, but we would probably have remained upright. Then there was the fact that Gert wasn't wearing a seat belt. Neither was I. We never had. Would that have made a difference? I thought of how Theresa had come forward just 15 minutes before the accident, and crawled into her

mother's arms. Would she be alive if she had stayed
back with Andy? As these thoughts pressed in on me,
I realized I couldn't bear them much longer.

It was so obvious as I reviewed the facts that God
could have spared us all. He could easily have let
us slide ten more feet, or delayed us or hurried us
up at the appropriate time. Or He could have taken
all four of us. All of these negative thoughts were
not from God. Satan was bombarding me with questions I couldn't answer. The contrast was glaring:
Satan burdened me with guilt; God bestowed on me
His peace. Satan's questions were a cancer that could
destroy me if not checked. I had to put my confidence in the supremacy of God who is all-knowing
and all-powerful and all-loving. I had to believe it
when He promised that "God causes *all things to work
together for good* to those who love God" (Romans
8:28 NASB). That promise answered all the
unanswerable questions.

In that light I thought again of the accident. It had
been so clean. Gert and Theresa didn't suffer at all.
They were killed instantly. Andy and I had been
spared. To me the conclusion was obvious. Though
I couldn't understand it, I knew God was sovereign.
And as I wept, I felt His tremendous peace flood over
me again. There was no guilt, because I had done
all I knew how to do at that time. If I had known
what I knew now, I would have acted differently.
But I didn't. I hadn't acted irresponsibly. Within the
pile of mail I had received was a letter from the man
who helped rescue Andy: "I found out who you were
from the newspaper...The road conditions were such
that the accident was unavoidable."

I could not understand why God had allowed this.
Perhaps I never would. But I knew that God was in
control because there were no loose ends, no
dangling threads. It happened so neatly, like a
surgeon making an incision with a sharp knife, so

that there is no infection or jagged edges. I continued to weep, but now they were tears of cleansing, for my conscience was clear. There were no feelings of resentment or bitterness. I knew enough of God to know that He was sovereign. He had created us and we had given our lives to Him. He had the right to take His children home whenever He wanted to.

That evening the incesant reviews and questioning that are the inevitable result of such a tragedy ended for me. It would have been fruitless to review the facts any further. To question them would only hinder God's healing work in my life. It had happened. Questioning wouldn't change that fact. It was time to focus on reality.

Already it was obvious that this event was touching many people around the baseball world. Every day I spent time going through letters and cards, but it was impossible to keep up with the flood of mail. The Indians brought over several mailbags full of letters addressed to me. Many were short, encouraging notes. "Andre, we're praying for you...We thank God for your witness...We're grieving with you in the loss of your wife and daughter." One man heard the news on a Christian radio station in Chicago and wrote to tell me how he had heard me speak and I had led him to the Lord several years ago. These notes uplifted me and let me know that there were thousands of people who were helping in some small way to bear my burden.

Other letters had an opposite effect. Some of them were exceedingly long. After reading a few lines, I had to lay them aside. These people felt a need to tell me all about their life histories and the loved ones they had lost and all the things they had tried to do to cope with their loss. I wanted to be polite, but I couldn't possibly read through all of them.

Some people sent me books and pamphlets on what to do when you lose a loved one. One woman

sent a rosary with a series of little prayers to repeat.
Several people sent memorials informing me that
they were praying for Gert. Some people sent pages
and pages of Scripture verses. Some felt compelled
to tell me what I had to do—your faith has to be
strong, or you need to search your life for sin and
cleanse it out, or you need to find a certain church
or person or book. These things didn't help me.
These people didn't understand. I wondered why
they felt they had to write me. They didn't realize
that God was in control. There was no way I could
have survived those first few days and weeks unless
He was in control. Only He could handle the devastation. I found no comfort in people telling me all the
things I needed to do. But I found great comfort in
baring my soul before Almighty God. The letters and
notes that meant the most were those that were short
and uplifting. I appreciated those people who cared
and were praying and simply wanted me to know
that.

There were other letters that were crying for help.
A newspaper reporter who had lost a 23-year-old son
wrote because he couldn't reconcile how God could
allow that. People were asking, "Does God really
care?" and "What's the purpose of death?" These
people were looking for some hope to cling to. They
were looking to me for answers, and I felt an obliga-
tion to try to help them.

But the only way I could help these people was
by directing them to the source of my comfort. I
thought often of my mother's exhortation from 1
Peter: "The Word of the Lord endures forever." After
reading a few letters, I inevitably turned to the Scriptures. I did read a few of the booklets that were sent,
but they didn't give me what I needed. The renew-
ing process came through the hours I spent each day
simply drinking in the soothing medicinal waters of
God's Word.

Paul's letter to the Philippians was particularly helpful. I read it and reread it many times in the weeks following the accident. It was a book of hope and joy in the midst of intense trial. Humanly speaking, the Apostle Paul was at his lowest point. He was in prison and his public ministry was over. Yet this was his most joyful letter. Every time I read those four short chapters, my spirit was revived. The principles that Paul taught were the key to helping me rebuild my life. Many a day I would weep before the Lord, then open this epistle and find comfort. I would read a few verses and meditate on them and pray them back to God.

It started in verse 3 of chapter 1, in which Paul said he thanked God in his every remembrance of the Philippians. I would stop and give thanks for Gert, for the wonderful wife and mother she was, for the fact that she loved the Lord and was with Him now.

Then Paul said, "I am confident of this very thing, that He who began a good work in you will perfect it until the day of Christ Jesus" (verse 6 NASB). I thanked God that His work was finished in Gert and Theresa, and that He was still working in me and would likewise complete His work in Andy and me.

I prayed along with Paul that my love "would abound still more and more" even though at this time I didn't feel any love. I prayed that, like Paul, my circumstances "would turn out for the greater progress of the gospel." Paul explained that though he was in prison, many people were responding to the gospel, beginning in Caesar's palace. I wanted to likewise proclaim Christ in the midst of my situation.

I felt along with the apostle the desire that Christ be exalted in my life and in Gert's life through her death. I felt the conflict Paul had when he desired to die and be with the Lord, yet also to live and continue to serve Him. I could say with Paul, "For me to live is Christ, and to die is gain...having the desire to depart and be with Christ...yet to remain in the flesh is more necessary."

As I finished reading chapter 1, I prayed that I would conduct myself in a manner worthy of the gospel of Christ. And I read that it had been granted for Christ's sake "not only to believe in Him, but also to suffer for His sake." I was beginning to understand that truth. So many of us athletes found it easy to believe God when things were going well. But God said that if we truly loved Him, we had to participate in Christ's sufferings also. I was seeing that through my suffering my faith was being purified. All that wasn't essential was being thrown out. What remained was the steadfast conviction that God was real, that He loved me, and that He had a purpose for my life. Suffering wasn't some morbid experience to be avoided at all costs. Christ had suffered, and as believers the only way we could begin to comprehend His love for us was to in some small manner experience a portion of His suffering.

During the times when Satan tried to invade my mind with guilt over the death of my wife, the first two verses of chapter 2 helped me deal with those thoughts: "If therefore there is any encouragement in Christ, if there is any consolation of love, if there is any fellowship of the Spirit, if any affection and compassion, make my joy complete by being of the same mind" (verses 1, 2 NASB). My hope came not through what the world offered but through what God says. The world tried to tell me that a person's spirit lives in our lives after death. Or that death meant the end of her existence. Or ideas like reincarnation. Or if one is good enough, surely she will enter heaven. None of these thoughts comforted. I was finding that the only thing I could set my mind on was His Word.

A good example of this truth was verse 13: "For

it is God who is at work in you, both to will and to work for His good pleasure'' (NASB). When I had surrendered my life to Christ at Fort Dix, and when Gert and I had totally dedicated our lives to Him in the Dominican Republic, we had given up the right to control our lives. He was at work in us, and He would do with us according to His good pleasure.

The fact was that if God was working in me for His pleasure, then in chapter 3, verses 7 and 8, I could say that whatever things were gain to me, those things I have counted as loss for the sake of Christ. In fact, Paul said: ''I count all things to be loss in view of the surpassing value of knowing Christ Jesus my Lord.''(NASB). It was almost easy to accept that now, because God had removed those people whom I considered my greatest gain. It seemed easy to consider everything else as loss.

Now God was calling me in chapter 3, verse 13, to forget ''what lies behind and reach forward to what lies ahead. I press on toward the goal for the prize of the upward call of God in Christ Jesus'' (NASB). What hope that upward call gave! ''For our citizenship is in heaven, from which also we eagerly wait for a Savior, the Lord Jesus Christ, who will transform the body of our humble state into conformity with the body of His glory'' (verses 20, 21 NASB).

With these powerful thoughts flooding my mind, it was almost easy to accept Paul's exhortation in chapter 4: ''Rejoice in the Lord always; again I will say, rejoice! Let your forbearing spirit be known to all men. The Lord is near. Be anxious for nothing, but in everything by prayer and supplication with thanksgiving let your requests be made known to God. And the peace of God, which surpasses all comprehension, shall guard your hearts and your minds in Christ Jesus. Finally, brethren, whatever is true, whatever is honorable, whatever is right, whatever is pure, whatever is lovely, whatever is of good repute, if there is any excellence and if anything worthy of praise, let your mind dwell on these things" (verses 4-8 NASB).

These verses gave me strength, so that I didn't just read later on that "I can do all things through Him who strengthens me" (NASB), but I knew it and experienced it. I had simply turned to God and He had produced the qualities of joy and peace in me. God's words were powerful and they were proven.

And so we approached the end of the year. Christmas Day came, and outside our living room window fresh snow clung to a spindly pine like a double layer of flock unevenly applied to a Christmas tree. The cold outdoors contrasted with the warm hearth as a fire crackled in the fireplace. Around me were the remains of Christmas wrappings, and the well-decorated tree looked bare without those packages underneath. Andy was playing quietly with one of his new toys while I silently reflected on the scene.

Several people had invited us to join them for Christmas, and my own family had encouraged us to come home. But we didn't want to be around anyone else. I didn't want people feeling sorry for us and hovering over us to try to make us happy. So we celebrated the birth of Christ alone, just the two of us. I knew it would be emotionally difficult, yet I felt we needed to pick up our lives and move on. It wouldn't help to postpone the adjustment that had to be made.

Christmas had always been a wonderful time for our family. We had many ornaments with special memories, and just the previous year I had taken movies of Gert and the kids decorating the Christmas tree and hanging the stockings. Actually, Gert did most of the work and the kids had scurried around her feet, enjoying the excitement. Unpacking those ornaments with Andy brought tears to my eyes.

As Andy dropped off to sleep, I laid him in his bed and gathered his toys together. As I stood there gazing at my son to whom I had become so intensely close during the past two months, I cried. These were not tears of total sorrow, but of hurt. This was a time when the loss of my loved ones penetrated deeply. I realized how I had lost my closest friend, the one person with whom I could share these precious moments.

But always the realities of God's Word held fast, even in these emotionally trying times. That was my foundation. I could be rocked and swayed by the emotional waves of the moment, but I could never be destroyed.

8

Can I Ever Love Again?

> Preserve me, O God, for I take refuge in Thee.
> I have said to the Lord, Thou art my Lord;
> I have no good besides Thee ....
> I have set the Lord continually before me;
> Because He is at my right hand,
> I will not be shaken.
> —Psalm 16: 1,2,8 NASB

The most common piece of advice I received in the weeks following the tragedy was "Don't worry; time heals all wounds." What was meant to be an encouragement did not encourage me at all, for in the devastation I seriously wondered whether I could ever again feel the same kind of love and happiness that I had experienced for seven years with Gert.

"I have set the Lord continually before me." There was my consolation. There was my hope for healing. There was my promise that there would be no damaging scars. There was my source of peace and strength in the midst of heartbreak.

During those weeks the psalms were a tremendous source of encouragement to me. They covered the full gamut of emotions. They expressed anger and frustration to God for the seeming injustices of this world, then remembered a soothing hope that ultimately His justice would prevail. The psalmists were allowed to express their emotions of fear and despair and depression, but always they returned to see God's design for creation.

Psalm 37 was particularly meaningful:

Do not fret because of evildoers,
Be not envious toward wrongdoers.
For they will wither quickly like the grass,
And fade like the green herb.
Trust in the Lord and do good;
Dwell in the land and cultivate faithfulness.
Delight yourself in the Lord,
And He will give you the desires of your heart.
Commit your way to the Lord,
Trust also in Him, and He will do it.
And He will bring forth your righteousness as
the light,
And your judgment as the noonday (verses 1-6
NASB).

Throughout this psalm there is a contrast between the righteous and the wicked. I could look around and see men who didn't have any love for God who were happily married. I could see many other men who were abusing their marriage relationships. But God took my wife, even though we were happily married and loved God and were serving Him. It didn't seem fair. Then I read, "For the Lord loves justice, and does not forsake His godly ones; they are preserved forever; but the descendants of the wicked will be cut off...But transgressors will be altogether destroyed; the posterity of the wicked will be cut off. But the salvation of the righteous is from the Lord; He is their strength in time of trouble."[1] Only by concentrating on God's Word could I gain the proper perspective. I had to look at God's long-range plans. In the short term life seemed unfair. But in the long term God's ways and God's people always prevailed.

Gradually, after many days of reading God's Word, my prayer times became more directed. Though just as intense as before, I was able to focus more clearly on the real needs and to pray intelligently for those needs. The most pressing demand was for my son. I knew I needed help in caring for Andy. During the first couple of months we had each other, and with a minimum of outside responsibilities we were able to spend most of our time together. We had grown extremely close and derived great comfort from each other. But soon spring training would arrive, and then there would be road trips. I knew someone would have to care for Andy during these times. So I prayed that God would provide a governess to help care for Andy.

I began to ask around, inquiring of Christians if they knew of an older woman or couple who might be willing to help. I had confidence that God would provide the right person, and so as I searched I was excited to find out how God would answer that prayer. Two couples were recommended and I scheduled interviews with them. One couple was Larry and Letha Byrd. They were middle-aged with a grown son. They loved the Lord, and I was confident after talking with them that they would help reinforce what I was teaching Andy. They moved into my home and I felt very comfortable leaving to do my workouts or other necessary jobs, knowing that Andy was cared for. So God provided richly in answer to this prayer.

Another specific area was my sexual drive. I asked God to quench my sex drive, even though since the accident I hadn't felt any sexual feelings whatsoever. But I knew myself well enough to know that someday those desires would return. I knew the temptations that came to professional athletes. I knew the women that hung around baseball teams. There would be opportunities on road trips to get into compromising situations, and I didn't want to do anything to disgrace the name of Christ. So I asked God to kill any sexual desires until He brought along someone to take Gert's place in my life. God was faithful in answering this prayer, too.

I also asked God to send me a friend. Though I was

drawing my total strength from the Lord, I felt the need for companionship, someone to talk to and have fellowship with. I needed a person with whom I could share all my pent-up thoughts and emotions. For the last few years that person, that friend, had been my wife. Now there was no one I could open up to. Howard Jones and I talked on the phone a couple of times, and he came over and prayed with me. But he was busy with his own ministry in the Billy Graham Evangelistic Association. There were other friends, but they all had ministries and families. I knew I needed someone I could call anytime of the day or night, someone who would help me think things through and who would pray with me. Little did I realize that Howard Jones would help provide the answer to that prayer.

But my greatest desire in prayer was that God would provide me with a wife. This I prayed without any real longing at first, for I seriously questioned if I could ever love another woman. I couldn't comprehend another relationship as sweet and wonderful as my relationship with Gert had been. But I knew I was a young man, not even 30 years old. I knew my son needed a mother. I knew God would provide for Andy's needs, but I also realized that he needed a woman to help raise him. I knew that the closest form of friendship and companionship came through marriage. And I knew my sexual desires would not remain curbed forever. So I prayed fervently that God would sent someone to me.

That prayer was intensified after I began receiving some not-so-subtle offers. Several times I received phone calls (though my number is unlisted) from women who suggested they were available. Several women wrote to me and appealed to the fact that I had ministered to them spiritually through my public witness. One nurse wrote me after I visited a nursing home where she worked. This was a special Christmastime visit, and I shared my faith with the patients. I talked with this woman briefly, and only concerning my relationship with Christ. She wrote to me and enclosed a picture. She stated that she knew God had sent me to that nursing home to meet her so I could become her husband.

All such calls were rejected, and I threw away those letters as quickly as possible. I was far too vulnerable. Some Christians might say I could trust God, and that He would protect me. While that was true, I still wasn't willing to let myself be tempted any more than necessary. There were too many men stronger than I who had compromised in this area and had hurt the cause of Christ. I did not want to dishonor the Lord. So I prayed with great intensity that God would send me a godly woman. I could not imagine waiting ten years for another mate. In this area I felt that God would have to act quickly.

But unlike my search for Andy's governess, I didn't feel confident in my ability to look for a wife. I couldn't comprehend dating different women and courting them and playing the frivolous games that young couples play. In my condition I couldn't trust my own judgment. So I prayed that God would bring this woman to me and place her in front of me so that there could be no question that He had provided her. This way, all my attention would be on Christ, and not diverted by searching for another woman.

Of all my prayers, these were some of the most precious. I knew that God heard my prayers and that He would provide for me in His own perfect timing. There was a conviction that God would not delay His answer for long.

One evening I was thinking about the things that had made our marriage so successful. Our communication was open and honest; we could talk about anything. I reflected on how Gert was willing to work as hard as I was to make our home and our career a success. I thought of the tenderness we shared, those intimate moments that we would never know again. Then I was drilled by the thought, "There is no marriage in heaven. I'll never know Gert in the same way." Depression swelled over me like a dark storm cloud, and I was overpowered. I knew that the Bible promised I would see Gert in heaven, but that would be a totally different relationship. It seemed so blunt. Our relationship as husband and wife was over—forever.

When I saw that I couldn't cope with these thoughts, I opened my Bible and read the passages from which this idea came. A group of the Sadducees, a Jewish sect that believed in rigid interpretation of the first five books of the Old Testament and also that there was no life after death, questioned Jesus. They presented Him with a hypothetical situation. A man married a woman and then died without having any sons. According to Jewish law, the man's brother was to take the woman as his wife and raise up a son to perpetuate the family line. This man had six brothers, and each of them took this woman as his wife, and each died without leaving an heir. Finally the woman died also. Their question was: "In the resurrection...whose wife of the seven shall she be? For they all had her."

Jesus answered them by saying, "You are mistaken, not understanding the Scriptures or the power of God. For in the resurrection they neither marry nor are given in marriage, but are like angels in heaven."[2]

First, Christ emphasized that these men didn't understand the Scriptures or God's power. Christ seemed to be saying that things are different in heaven. We would have new bodies. We would no longer be dominated by the physical needs and emotions we experience now. I thought about the angels. They spend their time worshiping God and serving Him. All their energies are focused in that direction.

Heaven wouldn't be like earth at all. It would be much better, so much so that we couldn't comprehend it now.

As I wrestled with this thought, I again felt God's peace. I would know Gert, but we would have a different relationship. My depression wasn't from God. The negative thoughts plaguing me were from our spiritual enemy, Satan. He wanted me to concentrate on my human loss rather than on my future joy. When I focused again on my hope in the Lord, I was immersed in His joy and felt content.

This was one example of how God's Word was not only healing me, but combating the barrage of questions and doubts that often assailed me. There were nights when I struggled with the reality of the hope I had for my wife and daughter. I had to determine whether to rest in my own unstable feelings or in what God told me was the truth in His Word.

> But I would not have you ignorant, brethren, concerning those who are asleep, that you sorrow not, even as others who have no hope. For if we believe that Jesus died and rose again, even so those also who sleep in Jesus will God bring with Him. For this we say unto you by the word of the Lord, that we who are alive and remain unto the coming of the Lord shall not precede those who are asleep. For the Lord Himself shall descend from heaven with a shout, with the voice of the archangel, and with the trumpet of God; and the dead in Christ shall rise first; then we who are alive and remain shall be caught up together with them in the clouds to meet the Lord in the air; and so shall we ever be with the Lord. *Wherefore comfort one another with these words.*"[3]

There was another question that occupied my mind for a long time: "What was God's purpose for this tragedy? What could I learn from it? How could He use it to bring glory to Himself?" I never did question God in removing Gert and Theresa. I didn't even have the right to challenge God's sovereignty. If I did, I couldn't have even continued to live, for there was no hope. But Romans 8:28 tells us that God causes all things to work together for good to those who love God. I wondered what the good was in this tragedy.

Job said, "When He has tried me, I shall come forth as gold."[4] The analogy seemed apt, since gold can only be refined by fire, and I felt like I was being burned. But it was a purifying process. "Consider it all joy," wrote James, "...when you encounter various trials, knowing that the testing of your faith produces endurance. And let endurance have its perfect result, that you may be perfect and complete, lacking in nothing."[5]

The Apostle Paul also made this point: "For I consider that the sufferings of this present time are not worthy to be compared with the glory that is to be revealed to us."[6] Peter talked about it too: "Therefore, since Christ has suffered in the flesh, arm yourselves also with the same purpose, because he who has suffered in the flesh has ceased from sin, so as to live the rest of the time in the flesh no longer for the lusts of men, but for the will of God...Beloved, do not be surprised at the fiery ordeal among you, which comes upon you for your testing, as though some strange thing were happening to you; but to the degree that you share the sufferings of Christ, keep on rejoicing; so that also at the revelation of His glory, you may rejoice with exultation."[7] And finally Peter says: "And after you have suffered for a little while, the God of all grace, who called you to His eternal glory in Christ, will Himself perfect, confirm, strengthen and establish you."[8]

The point seemed very clear in Scripture that God used our suffering to make us into the people He wanted us to be. It was like dross being skimmed from molten silver to make it pure. He was molding me, cutting out lustful desires, pride, anger—anything that was sinful. And He was doing it quickly, through radical surgery. This tragedy had seemingly accelerated the process that would lead to my being more effective for Him, and ultimately it would bring Him greater glory when He returned. In the midst of my grief, Psalm 30:5 was encouraging: "Weeping may last for the night, but a shout of joy comes in the morning" (NASB).

With all these promises flooding my mind, I thought about my message to the world. Already people were beginning to ask me questions. Reporters wanted to do interviews. Churches wanted me to speak. And once the season started, I knew the opportunities would increase. What would I tell these people?

An increasing burden to share the gospel was building within me. More than ever before, I wanted to tell everyone of the hope I knew in Christ. During the early days of the new year I read the book of Jeremiah. This faithful prophet proclaimed God's message to a generation that refused to listen. Many times, in many ways, he pleaded that Israel would return to the Lord and be spared of the judgment that would come in exile. I felt the urgency in Jeremiah, an urgency that could easily be transferred to our age. The people around me were living life as if there was no day of reckoning. They might pause for a moment to reflect on the death of someone in the public eye, even as they did in my situation. But the next moment it was suppressed. I had seen graphically how limited our time is on this earth. I had seen how quickly a life can be snuffed out. But many people wouldn't face this. They couldn't acknowledge that God would hold them accountable for their lives. If they did see it, few lived as if it made any lasting impression on their lifestyle.

Andre talks about his faith with prison inmates.

Sharing the Lord with teammate Pat Kelly.

Team Bible study during Indians spring training.

When I read the words of the Lord to Jeremiah—
"Before I formed you in the womb I knew you, and
before you were born I consecrated you; I have ap-
pointed you a prophet to the nations"[9]—I felt a
stirring within me that God had set me apart to help
proclaim His message to the United States. I could
only respond like the young prophet who said, "Alas,
Lord God! Behold, I do not know how to speak."[10]
God answered him, "Everywhere I send you, you
shall go, and all that I command you, you shall
speak"[11] and "Behold, I have put My words in your
mouth."[12]

God's message in Jeremiah was relevant today.
Change a few names and He could be talking to
California and New York rather than to Judah and
the other tribes of Israel. "Has a nation changed gods
when they were not gods? But My people have
changed their glory for that which does not profit.
Be appalled, O heavens, at this, and shudder, be very
desolate...For My people have committed two evils:
They have forsaken Me, the fountain of living waters,
to hew themselves cisterns, broken cisterns, that can
hold no water."[13]

So many people were putting their faith in
something of no value. They were worshiping
materialism and humanism and were ridiculing the
Bible as an outdated book full of myths. They didn't
realize that God said, "I am watching over My word
to perform it."[14] God's Word had proved its worth
and power in my life. I was being called not as a
preacher or a Bible teacher, but as a man who could
testify to the power of God's Word in my life.

Early in February I headed for San Diego to participate in a Pro Athletes Outreach conference.
Toward the end of that week, Arlis Priest, the presi-
dent of PAO, asked me to give the closing challenge
to nearly 100 NFL and major league baseball players.
It was an emotional time, and as tears came down
my face and those of many in my audience, I tried

to communicate to them some of my intense convictions:

I have a burden on my heart for the urgency of getting out the gospel and being the people Christ wants us to be. I came to this conference last year with Gert, my wife. Having been a Christian for 10 of the 11 years of my professional career, God took us up that ladder of growth year by year. We knew the true joy of two people living in Christ—stumbling and yet not stumbling; failing but not really failing. We have seen many athletes stand up for Christ, and yet their lives are not being the examples that Christ asked us to be. Last year as we met many of you, my prayer was, "Lord, help us see a revival, not only in our own lives, but also in our communities and the nation."

I pray that none of you will ever have to cross the valley that I've had to cross. Many things have happened that have knocked me to my knees. It's made me look around with a burden on my heart that some of you might not understand. There is an urgency of taking the Word of God and letting it abide in our hearts so that others might know that we are Christians. People, sometimes we walk around thinking that our life is a smile. Sometimes the Lord takes us through valleys where outwardly we can't smile but inwardly we have the satisfaction of living in Him. That smile is in our Christian walk. That smile is in our dependence on Him, knowing that we are as the dust of this earth to Him.

No longer can we be children. No longer can we think that because we have been taught we don't have a responsibility to get it out. Our world is not getting better, and especially in the United States. The depravity of man in this country is not decreasing but increasing. If we as Christians don't imbed in our hearts the reality of Jesus Christ, this world will never know revival. People, this burden is heavy on my life. We can bring about revival in this country. We can bring about revival in our neighborhoods and within our families.

As I finished my talk, Tom Graham, a linebacker for the Denver Broncos, came up and, with tears streaming down his face, threw his arms around me. Other athletes gathered around us, and it was evident that God had moved many of these men. God was confirming the ministry He wanted me to have. I was to share His love and abundant strength as demonstrated in my life. I was to encourage those who were hurting by showing them what God was doing in my life. And I was to exhort fellow believers to live a vital faith centered in God's Word.

Two weeks later it was time to leave for spring training. The pain from my loss was not over, though it had been four months. But I was able to function. I was experiencing the daily sustenance of God's grace. And I knew that God was definitely going to use this. There would be unique opportunities to speak out for Him. I went to camp knowing that I could trust God to answer my prayers and meet my needs and my son's needs. The healing process would continue, but meanwhile, it was time to begin seeing the results of God's work in my life.

Scripture References

1. Psalm 37:28,38-39 NASB.
2. Matthew 22:28-30 NASB.
3. 1 Thessalonians 4:13-18.
4. Job 23:10 NASB.
5. James 1:2-4 NASB.
6. Romans 8:18 NASB.

7. 1 Peter 4:1,2,12,13 NASB.
8. 1 Peter 5:10 NASB.
9. Jeremiah 1:5 NASB.
10. Jeremiah 1:6 NASB.
11. Jeremiah 1:7 NASB.
12. Jeremiah 1:9 NASB.
13. Jeremiah 2:11-13 NASB.
14. Jeremiah 1:12 NASB.

Reaping Joy

On this Easter morning, for a change of pace, I'd like to tell you a little bit about a man named Andre Thornton who'll be playing first base for the Indians at Fenway Park today.

He is quite obviously, an exceptional athlete, which means he has access to a large share of this world's earthly goods, not the least of which are fame and fortune far greater than most of us will ever know.

But more than that, the 29-year-old born-again Christian is a man of deep and abiding faith whose life has become an inspiration to kids and grown-ups alike, both in and outside of the ballpark.

His message is a simple one. "I'm sure some people come to hear me just because I'm an athlete," he says. "I've met people from all walks of life, from all over the country, and it doesn't take long to realize their needs are no different than mine. They can't cope with their problems, and they see no hope for the way their lives are going. Many times they're just waiting for someone to share with them the hope of Jesus Christ."

The key to coping, Thornton believes, is a proper arranging of life's priorities, which means the Almighty Dollar doesn't rank very high on his list.

"What in the world can be so important to me when I know that ultimately I must lose it?" he says. "Or tell me this: what does Howard Hughes have right now that I want?

"You see, I know what it's like to go through valleys in this life. There have been times I've been as low to the ground as I'll ever be, when I've looked and could not see the direction the Lord was taking me in. And yet I can honestly say that even in those moments I've felt a peace within my heart, because the Lord has said He'll never leave or forsake us, and I know that to be true."

—from "An Easter Story About an Athlete's
Faith"
by Joe Fitzgerald
Boston Herald American
April 15, 1979

Beginning in spring training, there was tremendous interest from the media about my tragedy and how I was coping. Everywhere I went, reporters wanted to talk with me. Most were cautious at first, not knowing quite how to approach this sensitive topic. They weren't sure whether it was appropriate to ask such personal questions. Perhaps if I had hit .220 with five home runs the previous year, they would have let it pass. But to them this was a major news story. So I tried to make them feel at ease, and I talked openly about how God had provided for me through the tragedy. Every reporter seemed sympathetic and most quoted me accurately. And they cooperated when I asked them, as a favor, to thank all the fans who had written to me during the past few months, since it was impossible to answer everyone personally.

Physically, I worked hard in camp, doing what now came almost instinctively after so many years in baseball. But mentally, I didn't feel ready to resume playing baseball. The game seemed so insignificant after what I'd been through. At times I was enticed by the thought that it was time to leave baseball and get into full-time Christian ministry, for the game seemed so meaningless in the light of life-and-death issues. But God made it clear that my ministry was in baseball, for I was still capable of playing several more years. My primary motivation for playing was to be used by God. The money and glory were insignificant compared to that goal. Fortunately, my message didn't fall on deaf ears.

When the tragedy occurred, my wife and I went to the funeral. It was the most moving experience of my life. My dad died two years before and I thought that was moving, but this was more so. Andre's beliefs came out and strengthened us all. He spoke and said that he was sad on the outside, but at peace on the inside. He said that before another life slipped away, he prayed that each one would find the Lord as he had.

My wife and I drove back, about a 2½-hour drive, and neither of us said much. We marveled at his strength. He's a special human being. Later, around Thanksgiving time, I decided to give him a call, hoping maybe I could boost his morale a bit. We spoke on the phone for 30 minutes. I think I talked about a minute and he spoke the other 29. And he strengthened me.

—Jeff Torborg, Cleveland manager, 1977-79

With the manager's blessing, I started a weekly Bible study in Tucson, as well as a daily prayer meeting. The response was encouraging, as 20 to 25 players and wives attended the studies. Part of it was probably because they realized that the tragedy could just as easily have happened to one of them. They were certainly open to hearing what the Word of God has to say. This did much to instill enthusiasm in me for the new season.

There were a few players who were uncomfortable around me and didn't know how to approach me. Some seemed to keep away, as if I was contaminated. They probably didn't realize that they were rejecting me, but I felt it. Some felt they had to say something and waited until we were alone. "I want you to know I'm really sorry about what happened," they would say. You could tell those who were genuinely concerned from those who were saying something only because they felt they had to.

Baseball locker rooms are usually a relaxed place where players expend a lot of creative energy kidding each other. After a while some of the guys let it be known that I was too serious, especially about my faith. It was true; I was serious. I felt an urgency about life that most of them couldn't understand. My faith was a life-and-death issue to me.

One afternoon before a night game in Anaheim against the Angels one of our pitchers asked if we could talk privately. I knew that this player was having marital struggles, but when we talked I learned that it was even more serious than that, for he also admitted having a drinking problem. He was in his second marriage and it was failing. He seemed desperate, to the point that to me he seemed on the verge of suicide. "Andre, I can't go to anyone else," he said. "You're like a pastor. I thought you'd understand." This man who looked so successful on the outside had a gaping wound on the inside. He didn't need a Band-Aid, he needed sutures.

This was not the only teammate who came to me privately that season, though he was the most distraught. Some players, when they were struggling with personal problems, felt I would understand and offer some help. My answers weren't always accepted, but at least they listened. They confirmed that it was far more important to be available to them with respect to eternal matters than to feel obliged to play locker room games to perhaps gain momentary popularity.

Buddy Bell and I flew to the funeral on our own. We simply wanted to be by his side. And I'll tell you something: in all of my 28 years on this earth, I have never seen or felt anything as traumatic as that service. Buddy felt the same way. It obviously takes a strong individual to get through something like that, and down deep neither one of us had any doubt that Andy had that kind of strength. People were already asking whether or not the man would ever play again, but I can remember Buddy and I sitting together on the plane that day, heading back to Cleveland, agreeing that if anybody could do it, Andy could.

Baseball's not your normal lifestyle. The greatest publicity usually goes to the guys who spend all night drinking, then hit two or three homers the next afternoon. So it's not an easy area for a guy like Andy to witness about Jesus Christ, as he puts it. In baseball you have to live with the same 30 or so people for seven and eight months at a time, working together, traveling together, being together.

Andy lets everyone know what his beliefs are, and he makes himself available to any of us who might want to discuss with him, but he doesn't force those views on anyone else. It's a different kind of leadership than you usually hear about, but he's definitely a leader, if only by example.

—Duane Kuiper, Indians' captain, 1978

On the field, I got off to my typical slow start. My game didn't begin to warm up until the weather did in June. Then my batting average rose and the home runs and RBIs started coming in clusters. Unfortunately, our team struggled on the field, unable to reach even the .500 level.

If there was any temptation to revel in my success, it quickly fell back into perspective during the final weekend series at home. On Sunday morning, September 24, we read about the death of Lyman Bostok, an outstanding player for the California Angels. He had accidentally been shot to death by a man who was trying to kill his estranged wife. Said a policeman at the scene of the accident, "Lyman was at the wrong place at the wrong time."

That day our clubhouse chapel service was packed as almost every player on the team attended. We prayed for Lyman's wife and family and I shared with the team about how they could know for sure they were going to heaven when they died.

I felt led to give an invitation, and several players indicated decisions to follow Christ. It was a touching time for many of us on the team.

But the next day some players weren't taking it quite so seriously. A couple of guys joked about it and implied that Lyman had brought his death on himself by "fooling around." I couldn't understand their attitude. It might just as easily have been one them.

(Less than a year later Yankee catcher Thurman Munson was killed in the crash of a small plane. No one laughed this time, because everyone could see that no one is immune from death. No one wants to admit it, especially when he is young and healthy. But God doesn't always give us 70 years to determine what we're going to do about Him.)

About this time the announcement was made that I had won the Danny Thompson Award for exemplary Christian spirit in baseball. This was a tremendous honor, for it showed me that people were truly seeing God work through my life. The award was named in honor of Danny Thompson, who had played for the Minnesota Twins and Texas Rangers before he died of leukemia in 1975. Two years before his death he accepted Christ and had a dramatic impact on his teammates (including my current teammate, Mike Hargrove) and all of baseball.

We finished our season in New York against the Yankees. My final hit of the year was a two-run home run against Catfish Hunter to help send the Yankees to a defeat and force a sudden-death playoff for the division title between Boston and New York. That home run gave me 33 for the year and 105 RBIs, the most on the team and fourth best in the American League in both categories.

One week later I flew to Los Angeles for the Thompson Award ceremony, but my plans were

changed at the last minute because of the death of
"Junior" Jim Gilliam, a coach for the Dodgers. Junior
was buried the morning of the second game, and I
was in attendance at the funeral.

Junior was an outstanding second baseman for the
Dodgers in the 1950's and '60's, then became one
of the team coaches. He was respected by people
throughout baseball. The Dodgers dedicated their
pennant to the man and wore black patches with his
number "19" on the uniforms during the World
Series in his memory.

The funeral was almost a pageant, with Dodger
stars past and present attending. More than 2000
people crammed Trinity Baptist Church, and more
crowded around outside, many with cameras to snap
pictures of the sports celebrities like basketball great
Bill Russell and Hall of Fame pitcher Sandy Koufax.

There were six men who eulogized Jim, including
Dodger captain Dave Lopes and Reggie Jackson of
the Yankees. They all mentioned how great he was.
Most of them said his spirit would remain with them.
One man questioned why God would want to take
someone like Junior Gilliam when there are so many
wretched people in the world. Reggie seemed to be
the only one who held any sort of hope. "When I
learned of Jim's death Sunday," he said, "I asked
God through Jesus Christ to explain why He took
Jim. He decided that now was the best time to take
him, with the World Series and everyone watching
and listening, so all God's children could take a look
at Jim and see what his life meant to us all."

My heart was moved by the service, not because
of the man Jim Gilliam, but because there were 2000
people there, most of whom didn't have any hope.
Perhaps at this service they could find the answer.

The main speaker was a well-known black
preacher who was famous for his political activism.
He talked about Junior and all of his talents, and how

Sue Ogrocki

Andre Thornton hit 33 home runs in 1978.

he had been deprived of the opportunity to be a manager in the big leagues. He tried to comfort the audience with these words: "Today the whole world knows Jim Gilliam. The comfort that we must take is knowing that part of living is dying. Each of us has a date with destiny and a rendezvous with eternity. Most of us cannot be famous. But all of us can be great. Jimmy was famous and great."

Never once did this preacher indicate what people should do about their "rendezvous with eternity." I was distressed that this man, a reverend who would logically be expected to have a message from God, didn't have anything to say. There was no real comfort, nothing to offer people hope, no answers to their questions. It seemed most of those 2000 people walked away sadder than when they came. At best, they didn't even remember what the preacher had said. A golden opportunity to share the gospel was missed.

That afternoon during a press conference where the starting pitchers for the game that night were introduced, I was presented with my award. I thought of Paul when he said to Timothy, "God has not given us a spirit of timidity, but of power and love and discipline. Therefore do not be ashamed of the testimony of our Lord" (2 Timothy 1:7,8 NASB). I briefly thanked the Baseball Chapel organization that made the award and said, "In my 12 years in baseball, the Lord has brought about in my life a gradual change in growth and strength. I pray that this will continue. I just want the reality of Jesus Christ to show in my life. That's what this award means to me."

Later that off-season I was presented with the Cleveland Man of the Year Award, as voted by the Cleveland Chapter of the Baseball Writers Association of America. But the biggest surprise came in

*Teammates congratulating Andre after another
home run.*

early 1979, when I was named winner of the annual Roberto Clemente Award. The nominees are chosen on the basis of sportsmanship, character, community involvement, humanitarianism, playing ability, and contributions to their teams and to baseball. The winner is chosen by a panel of baseball executives and members of the media. Previous winners included Willie Mays, Brooks Robinson, Al Kaline, Willie Stargel, Lou Brock, Pete Rose, Rod Carew, and Greg Luzinski. I felt truly honored to be included among such all-star company.

The award was presented by baseball commissioner Bowie Kuhn at a luncheon in Cleveland. I was invited to make an acceptance speech, which was printed verbatim the next morning in the Cleveland paper.

It's indeed a humbling and very gratifying and wonderful experience to be standing here before you as recipient of this great award, when I think of the people who have received the award and when I think of the man for whom this award is given.

I only met Roberto Clemente once in my life. I had the opportunity to see him play on the field at various times, and certainly as a ball player I could never reach the goals that this man attained. His ability was awesome, and not in my wildest dreams could I possibly say that I could fill his shoes on a ball field. But I am thankful that this man's life to us was something more than just the things he was able to do on a baseball field.

I won't remember Roberto Clemente for the fact that he was probably one of the greatest players that will ever play this game. I will remember that he gave his life giving, and helping, and serving other people.

I think of my own life in the same terms, considering the things that are really important. I have been gifted with the ability to play baseball, and I am thankful that I have been able to do it at times well—thankful that I have had the opportunity to play here before you in Cleveland, and hopefully be representative of you and this community.

And as I think about the things that I could possibly do in my life that would let you know how much I care for you, the only thing that I could possibly have to give you is not what I could do for you on the baseball field, but to give you my life. When I think of giving you my life, I think of sharing what Christ has done for me. The people I talk to, the people that question me, the people that want to know, "Andre, how can you make it? What gives you the strength to go on?" very seldom ask me how many home runs I hit last year.

It's almost forgotten in their minds simply because there's a problem much deeper than the one baseball can answer. The people who come to me are the people who are hurting, people who want to know if there is any hope, people that want to know, "How can I stand?" "Can this life offer me any enjoyment?" "Is there a purpose for this life?" I want to be able to share with people that there is hope; to encourage people that there is a purpose to this life; to encourage people in a time that, as the commissioner said, is very sinister. I think it is imperative that I not only be the best baseball player I can possibly be for you—because that is my job—but that I also be the man that God wants me to be, because that's what He demands. If I could ever do anything in this life for the Lord, it is to live in obedience to His Word. For there is nothing that brings a greater joy, and there is nothing that gives greater understanding.

The 1979 season saw my worst start ever. For a while I struggled to manage one hit in ten at-bats. But still the opportunities for witness were abundant. *Sport* magazine did a feature article, as did *Baseball* magazine. *Decision* and *Guideposts* both featured my testimony. Newspapers across the country asked me to talk about my struggle on the field from a Christian perspective.

Letters continued to flow in from around the country as God showed me how He was blessing His Word. I even received a letter from Ghana, from someone who read my article in *Decision*. He wrote that the article "made so much impact on me that I feel obliged to drop these few lines seeking a favor. As Christian as you are, I am convinced that it may please you to help a needy believer get answers to the questions that still agitate my mind: What is life? Why am I here? Where am I going? I am very much interested in getting firsthand information on how you answer the questions above."

Another letter came to me from a prison inmate: "I know you don't know me but I swear after I read the story in this magazine, I was really impressed with the way you handle yourself. I just wanted to have someone to write. I only have one person who cares about me and that's my grandfather, but he's in a rest home."

Another letter came to me from a university professor who read an article about me in *The Sporting News*. "Although I have been an ardent baseball fan for most of my 32 years, this is the first letter I've ever written to a professional ball player. What really overwhelmed me was a paragraph towards the end of the article which described how you were able to continue to praise the Lord despite the tragedy that occurred in your life. When I read this, tears filled

Ron Kuntz

One of many opportunities to share in the Cleveland area and around the country.

Andre receiving the Danny Thompson award from Craig Reynolds, 1978.

my eyes and I said to myself, 'There is a man who has really put his trust in the Lord.' I am greatly encouraged by hearing this sort of thing. Until three months ago I was a rebel against God and for most of the time the past 12 years I was an atheist... Through this letter I want you to know that there are those of us who support you in our prayer that you use your life as a baseball player as a living testimony to the reality of the Lord.''

A college student from Kansas wrote this: ''I just read the article about you in *Sport* last night. It was a great uplift to hear how God was working in your life. Also the boldness with which you share your beliefs gives me more strength to do likewise. Although Christ is our example, it is so encouraging to hear that someone is as great a witness to a ball team and a city as you.''

Once again, I managed to improve on the field during the second half and finished with 26 home runs to lead the Indians for the third straight year. I was satisfied to be able to recover and play well, but my joy came from the fact that God had taken an average player with no national reputation and given him an opportunity to spread His Word to millions of people. The letters gave me a glimpse of how he was using my life. I couldn't take credit for it. The results were the work of God, and of a unique woman who was willing to lay her life on the line so that God might use her in a significant way. This wasn't a record of what Andre Thornton had done. It was a tribute to the life of Gertrude Thornton and to our great God.

> It was raining when I woke yesterday morning and I thought of Andre Thornton. I thought of him because a week ago in Cleveland, while they were waiting for the rain to stop so the baseball game could go on, I spent an hour talking with him; a most remarkable hour. I have thought of him often since

then I have been touched by Andre Thornton.

I had never talked with him before, not really. I knew him as a powerfully built athlete who could crunch a baseball, and my conversations with him were the typical questions asked of a star whose home run has just won a game.

"What pitch did you hit? Have you always had good success against Catfish Hunter? Is this the biggest home run of your career?"

But I had never talked with Andre Thornton before. I knew about the tragedy in his life. I had read about how he and his family had been driving on a rain-slicked highway when the accident occurred. His wife and two-year-old daughter were killed. Andre and his four-year-old son survived. My heart went out to him in his grief and I said a quick, silent prayer that he could find peace and understanding in his bereavement, and I subsequently read that he had picked up the pieces of his life and I admired him for it.

I wondered how he had found the strength to carry on, but how do you find the right words to ask a man to discuss how he repaired the broken pieces in his life? Andre Thornton made it easy.

He was sitting in front of his locker, reading a newspaper and waiting for the rain to stop. The paper had been filled with tragedy, reports of the DC-10 crash in Chicago, another story about an Ohio man who had played Russian roulette with his four-year-old son, putting a gun to the child's head and pulling the trigger, killing his son.

"So many people don't realize the brevity of life," he said. "Those 272 people on that airplane might have had two minutes during which they knew they were going to die. We're going to have to answer that question. What is life all about? Where am I going? Am I going to have to stand before God?"

He was speaking softly, with great feeling, and I got the inescapable feeling that I was in the presence of a very special human being.

"When my wife and daughter were killed," he

said, "I knew I couldn't possibly understand the reasons for such a tragedy. There was nothing humanly anyone could do to heal the severed lives that were picked up that day.

"My faith in Christ brought me through this thing. I couldn't have found the strength without having faith and knowing this is God's will. Gert (his wife) and I had known the Lord all our married years. I can remember her saying God uses our lives and she wondered how He was going to use her. Now she knows how God has used her life."

I was enraptured as he spoke, with deep emotion, at peace. "I never experienced more pain, nor would I ever experience more pain," he said. "I'm just thankful I knew God, to be able to trust in Him. I believe my beliefs and I suspect my doubts. I certainly could pray, and that's what I did....

"I look at these games as a job," he says. "Put next to the things that are eternal, it doesn't mean much. If it meant that God wants me to leave this game, I would. I'm just an average ball player. I'm not looking to be in the Hall of Fame. This is where God has chosen to use me, and I put as much effort and as much love as I can in what I do.

"I'm serving the Lord by playing baseball. It allows me to reach more people. I believe that God does things to strengthen us and to test us. The tragedy in my life was meant to do that, and as a result I received thousands of letters from people who have been touched and affected by my tragedy. It humbled me."

When I left Andre Thornton, knowing I had been touched by this man and that I would never be the same, he said to me: "I will pray for you."

I have been associating with athletes for more than 20 years. Not one of them has ever said that to me before.

—from "Thornton, a Remarkable Man of Faith"
by Phil Pepe
New York Daily News
June 4, 1979

10

Love Rekindled

For an instant the woman being introduced reminded me of Gert. She was petite and pretty. Her shoulder-length black hair framed a delicate, oval-shaped face. Her smile was warm and friendly as she said "Hello," then resumed helping her mother prepare dinner. Her name was Gail Jones, the 30-year-old daughter of Howard and Wanda Jones.

As I rejoined my host in the cozy antique drawing room of Howard's victorian-style house, the momentary warmth I had felt faded. I was emotionally drained, unable to appreciate an attractive woman. It was two days before Christmas, and Howard had invited me to join his family and a couple of his friends for dinner. In the two months since the tragedy, I had filled a few speaking engagements, but this was my first strictly social gathering, and I wasn't convinced that I was ready for it.

I had accepted Howard's invitation because I respected his work as an evangelist and the fact that he had walked with the Lord for 40 years. I wanted—indeed needed—to be around men like him. But at the same time I could be content in the solitude of my own home. I was quiet and uptight, unable to enter into much conversation.

As the evening wore on and we ate dinner and saw slides of the family's missionary activity in Africa, I began to relax and was thankful for the hospitality. I could see how much I needed human companionship. Still, I was anxious to be alone again. Only after I returned home did I realize that I desired more of that fellowship. Since the Jones family had been kind enough to invite me to dinner, I decided to reciprocate. I called them and arranged for their family to come to my home for a Sunday afternoon meal between Christmas and New Year's.

Though some of my neighbors had dropped by in the past two months, often to leave something for Andy and me to eat, this was the first time I had entertained anyone. Without my wife it felt awkward. I greeted the Joneses at the door—Howard and Wanda and their son David and two of their four daughters, Lisa and Gail—then resumed dinner preparations in the kitchen. Without a hostess, my guests were left alone, and they occupied themselves by exploring my house and examining the books in my library.

Finally, Wanda suggested that Gail check to see if she could assist me in the kitchen. As Gail worked over a pot of vegetables, she again reminded me of Gert. The pink sweater and green plaid wool slacks were clothes my wife might have chosen. But what especially attracted me was her spirit. I sensed a warmth and a tenderness. It was as if she understood my grief and was waiting for the appropriate opportunity to help. There was a oneness of spirit with her, even though we had yet to speak to each other, that I had not felt with anyone besides my son in recent weeks.

For some time now, I had prayed intently about the need for a friend. As I saw God meet my most intimate needs in the midst of my grief, I felt an ever-increasing joy, even as I shed tears over my human loss. I wanted to share that joy with someone else, and as I prayed, expressing that desire, I felt a certainty that my prayer pleased God and that He would answer it quickly.

I was aware of the fact that Gail was a mature woman, about my age. Her father had told me about the singing group she was in with her sisters Cheryl and Phyllis. They were known as the Jones Sisters and had cut four albums. I was aware of her rich Christian background and the ministries in which she had participated. Even now, as a flight attendant, she still devoted much of her time to singing for the Lord.

Was this the friend God wanted me to have? She was single. Since she lived in Chicago, any relationship would of necessity be primarily by phone. That, I thought, would make it easier at first, for there would be no pressure to pursue a romantic relationship. As a woman, she would probably better understand my desire to talk at this time in my life. But I wanted to confirm these impressions. I needed to know where her heart was. Since we would all be sitting down for dinner in a few minutes, there wasn't much time that we would be alone together.

It had been nearly ten minutes and neither of us had talked. My first question caught both of us by surprise. "What are you looking for in a man, a potential mate?" I could tell immediately from her eyes that she was vulnerable. She was willing to be open, perhaps almost welcomed it. In any other situation, the question would be considered presumptuous, yet at this moment it was our way of testing to see if perhaps God had brought us together for something more than just fixing dinner.

"I want someone who loves the Lord as much as I do," she answered softly. "I want a man who is committed to the Lord's work. And also, I would like to continue my singing ministry."

As we continued to prepare the meal and set the table, we talked quietly about our upbringing and how God was working in our lives. Then right before dinner was served I stopped working, turned to Gail, and said, "I really need a friend. Will you be my friend?" I could see tears welling up in her eyes as she answered, "Sure, I'll be your friend."

We had a wonderful dinner together that afternoon, with good conversation around the table. I felt comfortable now with the Jones family, especially with no other people around. Before we knew it, darkness was beginning to fall and Howard announced that he had a plane to catch early the next morning.

As the family prepared to leave, Howard suggested that we hold hands in a circle while he prayed for Andy and me. Gail was to my immediate right, and as we joined hands I again felt her warmth. Suddenly I was like a teenage kid holding his girl friend's hand for the first time; and I didn't want to let go. Only reluctantly did I release it after Howard had said "Amen."

At the door, I told Gail that I was planning to be in Chicago the last week of January for a Founders' Day program at Moody Bible Institute. Dr. J. Vernon McGee was speaking and I planned to hear him and then meet him afterward for dinner. If she wasn't working, perhaps she could join me. Gail said she would have to check her flight schedule, and she gave me her phone number and address.

That evening I experienced a sadness and void. For the first time I didn't want to be alone. Within what I thought was a dead heart was a spark of life. I didn't know how strong that spark was, but I was eager to find out. Still basking in the warmth of that moment, I wrote Gail a letter. "I hope you won't feel I'm taking anything for granted," I said. "But when I held your hand, I sensed that you felt what I felt. I believe you are someone I can talk to. Let's not kid each other. We're adults. I need your friendship. I need someone with whom I can be open and honest and who will be open and honest with me."

It was one month between our dinner and my trip

to Chicago, and most of those days were like the previous months, filled with the pain of my loss. Many memories still flooded my mind and more tears were shed. I continued to spend hours reading the Scriptures and praying. I still questioned whether I could ever be happy again. But now there was a ray of hope. Twice Gail and I talked on the phone, and in those long conversations I sensed again that oneness of spirit. She was willing to listen for hours as I poured out the emotions I was feeling and the way that God was ministering to me.

Our first date at the Founders' Day program was exciting, yet also an acute reminder of the fact that I was a widower who no longer fit into the normal social life of married couples. It didn't help when I was introduced by the emcee as a member of the Cleveland Indians who was taking correspondence courses from the school. After the program, many people—most of the them baseball fans—stopped to talk to us. They would introduce themselves and expected me to introduce my wife. A couple of them even said, "And this must be your wife." Since I knew the position that Gail and her family held in the Christian world, I felt I had to explain that this was Gail Jones, my friend.

But as we talked further, they would learn that I had a son, and then to avoid any misunderstandings, I felt I had to explain that my wife and daughter had been killed in an accident. Toward the end of the evening it was a struggle to handle it gracefully, and I was glad when we could slip away to meet Dr. McGee at his hotel coffee shop.

I had eagerly anticipated this meeting, hoping that Dr. McGee could provide some objective counsel. I was particularly interested in what he would say about Gail. I needed to know if it was all right to have feelings for her so soon after the tragedy.

Dr. McGee immediately recognized her. "I know

your father very well," he said when I introduced her. The Jones Sisters had sung at the Church of the Open Door in Los Angeles, where Dr. McGee had been pastor for many years. Later in the evening, when Gail excused herself for a few minutes, Dr. McGee told me that he thought she was "a very exceptional young lady. She comes from a good family. She'll be a stabilizing influence and will help you in your Christian life." And then he leaned over the table and with a twinkle in his eye said, "And besides that, she is really a good-looking girl!"

Dr. McGee's encouragement was what I needed. Though I knew that the need was great, and that I had prayed about it fervently, I had still wondered if it was right to pursue this relationship. But even more important, I didn't want to enter into a relationship where there was no hope. This encouragement conclusively demonstrated to me that God was answering my prayers.

Soon after that I headed to spring training and did not see Gail again for two months, though we talked on the phone every day. One night we talked for six hours. These conversations were the highlight of my day. There was freedom to discuss anything, from the events of the day, to baseball, to the details of Gail's trips and a new album she was cutting with her sisters.

Most of our time was spent talking about the Lord and what he was teaching us through the Scriptures. Usually we had daily devotions together. One of us would read a passage and then we would discuss it. We always ended our time with prayer, committing to God all the activities and needs of the day.

As we talked, my enthusiasm for how God was working grew. The emotions that were bottled up began to overflow. God's peace and joy that had guarded me in the weeks of grief were now flowering into new, fuller emotions. Often I felt incapable of expressing the joy I felt surging within me, and the only statement I could utter was "O, wow!" There didn't seem to be words that could adequately convey the goodness of God that I experienced.

One night during spring training I asked Gail to consider becoming a part of Andy's life and mine. It wasn't a formal proposal for marriage, but a definite step into a deeper relationship. "I'm not fooling anyone," I told her. "I need you. I need a mother for Andy. I was happy with Gert before and I want that happiness to continue for both myself and my son." Gail was very receptive, and from that point we prayed together that God would direct the development of our relationship.

A few weeks after the season opened, Gail was transferred by her airline to Cleveland, and she moved back home with her parents. But because of our schedules, our relationship still consisted primarily of phone conversations. I would occasionally make the two-hour drive out to Oberlin to see her, and sometimes we would meet for a few minutes in the parking lot after a ball game. Any time we could manage together was precious.

I found Gail a perfect sounding board for struggles and questions that I was wrestling through in my mind, even in baseball. While having my normal early-season hitting struggles, one of our clubhouse men suggested that I consider using a cork-filled bat. That's where the barrel of a bat is hollowed out and filled with cork. The end of the bat is then replaced and made to look normal. Since I use a black bat, the man convinced me that it would be virtually impossible to detect the deception.

Cork-filled bats made the ball more lively when hit, and several players used them. The only problem was that they are illegal. Still, I started using them and hit two long home runs, though my batting average did not improve. But my conscience made me uneasy.

One evening I told Gail about it. She wasn't very familiar with baseball—she admitted that football was her favorite sport—so I had to explain what a cork bat was and why I liked it. "Andre, what would happen if one of those bats cracked?" she asked. I told her that I would be ejected from that game and fined by the league. It would undoubtedly hurt my witness, since I was known for my public stand as a Christian.

"The Lord gave you 28 home runs last year without any help," Gail said. "And you have hit home runs before without any extra help. So why do you need a cork bat? If the Lord wants to give you 30 home runs, you'll get 30 home runs without cheating."

Gail's encouragement helped me make the decision to destroy those bats. And it showed me how much she had to offer my life. I admired her spirited personality, expressed in a willingness to speak her convictions. Yet at the same time she was gentle and sensitive and understanding. She had strength of character built through her hard-working, well-disciplined family. I could see it in her music, a desire for perfection that drove her to rehearse and practice a single song for hours until it was right. As an athlete, I respected that. I could see that determination as an asset in my home. By the end of May I had decided to ask Gail to marry me, and on June 1, her birthday, I presented her with an engagement ring.

I knew that many people would not understand our decision to marry so soon after the tragedy, and we delayed a public announcement until we had been seen together for a while longer. But I did not question our engagement, for I knew how intense our time with the Lord had been. I had asked God to bring the right person to me, and it was obvious that He had done just that. God had prepared Gail to be my wife.

For several years Gail had prayed about a husband. Her standards were high and she refused to compromise them, even when she found herself 30 years old with no prospects in sight. She remained confident that the Lord would provide a husband for her, though she suspected it might be through unusual circumstances.

Gail told me about a discussion she had had the previous October with a friend in the airlines. Over coffee they had discussed their futures, and Gail had shared her belief that God would provide a husband. Her friend raised the normal objections—that her standards were too high and that most men her age were either married or divorced. Then she posed this hypothetical question: "What if the Lord sends you a widower who has a young son?" She specifically remembered the reference to a son rather than to a child or daughter. It wasn't a question that many young women ever considered, but she answered that she felt she could handle it. "I would ask the Lord to help me love the son as my own child."

Three days after that discussion, Gail's mother called to tell her about the death of my wife and daughter and how Howard was getting together with us for prayer. Wanda had told Gail about me when Howard spoke to the Indians' chapel service the previous month, but she hadn't paid much attention. The news of the tragedy was a shock, and Gail found herself unable to clear her mind of this man and his son whom she had never met. So in those two months before the Christmas dinner at her parents' house, she prayed often for Andy and me. Now we realized that this was one of God's special ways that He prepared Gail for me.

There were other, more specific ways that Gail was

prepared for our family. My travel schedule during baseball season meant that I would be away from home a total of three months each year. While that would be difficult, Gail understood what it would be like because her father traveled while she was growing up. He was often away from home for six weeks or two months at a time. Wanda had set a strong example for raising a family in the absence of her husband. Gail felt that her mother's example would help her to cope when I was away.

Andy was excited about our relationship and felt comfortable asking her if he could start calling her "Mommie" several months before our marriage. He was so responsive to Gail's love and affection. I rejoiced that God had protected him, for there didn't seem to be any lingering scars in his life. I felt that Gail's background would help Andy. She had learned many creative ways of teaching Christian principles. When her family had lived in Liberia, she had helped produce a children's radio show with her sisters and had gone with the family out to the villages to conduct special Sunday school programs. So as I evaluated the many facts, I *knew* that God had brought us together.

One afternoon I invited Gail to my home and showed her pictures and films of Gert and Theresa. This was a difficult moment for both of us, but I felt Gail needed to know these two loved ones. I took her through our scrapbooks and showed her the movies I had taken of the family. Though that part of my life was over now, they would always be a part of my past. I could never forget them. Gail understood that, but still it was a struggle. With tears she told me of the guilt she sometimes felt because she was taking another woman's place. Gert and I had been so happy together, she told me, and she wondered why God would choose to take such a dear one home. Yet she also knew that God had prepared

her for this and had brought us together. She re
minded me that she was not Gert. She could not be
someone else, and I could not expect things to be ex-
actly as they were when I first married.

One of my biggest concerns was for Gert's family, and particularly her parents. I felt a responsibility to let them know about Gail and my plans
to remarry. So I arranged for Chick and Hazel to fly
to Cleveland. I didn't tell them why, and I know that
hurt Hazel. But I didn't believe she would come if
she knew the reason ahead of time.

The Thomases were in my backyard when Gail
came to my home after work. They obviously felt
comfortable with me, and Chick was doing some
yard work, trimming the hedges, while Hazel relaxed and enjoyed the sunny weather. When Gail
came by the house, I introduced her. I explained how
much I loved them both. "You will always be like
second parents to me. That's why I want you to be
the first to know." Hazel was shocked and unable
to say anything. Chick broke the tension, like I knew
he would, and said he was happy for both of us.

We didn't see them again until after we were married. But every time we go to Pennsylvania we visit
them. Hazel has made such an effort to get to know
Gail. We make sure that they know I am still their
son-in-law, and Andy spends a week or two with
them every summer and calls them frequently during the school year.

Gail and I went into our marriage knowing that
we would face some unusual adjustments. Gail
would not have time to grow into her new role as
wife and mother. As soon as we got home from the
honeymoon she would be helping to care for a six-
year-old boy. Even though Andy loved Gail, he was
a typical boy, and Gail would have to learn that
sometimes boys have to be reminded several times
to clean their rooms or do their homework or eat

Ron Kuntz

All three of us were convinced God had brought us together.

their vegetables, and she could not take that as a personal rejection.

Gail had never had to maintain more than a small apartment, but now she would be managing a 4000-square-foot house. We would not have time for lots of carefree fun, with dinners for two in candlelit restaurants and all the other romantic activities that newlyweds enjoy during their first year of marriage, when they just have each other.

She realized that she was marrying in a fishbowl setting, with the people of Cleveland looking on. There were still thousands of letters in the house waiting to be read and answered. The newspapers and radio and TV would be reporting me during the season, and would constantly remind us of the past. Even if we wanted to leave the tragedy behind us, we would invariably see those articles about Andre Thornton "whose wife and daughter were killed when the van he was driving skidded on a patch of ice and...."

There was a lot of work to be done. For me, probably the hardest adjustment was realizing that we were starting over. I couldn't just plug Gail into my family and resume where we left off in October of 1977. She was a unique and special woman whom God had brought into our lives to help us with the task at hand. But it would take time for us to get to know each other, and for her to fit into new roles. I would have to learn to be sensitive, to give her a little flower when she needed encouragement, or to make time in our busy schedule for a romantic dinner for two, or to do some of the household chores when she felt buried by all the work. My excitement and enthusiasm for doing these things came from knowing that God had brought us together. And since I knew that God had brought us together, I knew that He would also sustain us and provide all the resources we needed to accomplish the job.

Our wedding day was another blessing. We were married on November 4, 1978. It was a crystal-clear day with a temperature of 70 degrees, almost unheard-of weather for November in Ohio. To us it was like God saying, "This is something I have done." Just as a summer day in November was a miracle, so our whole relationship was a miracle. God had intervened and rekindled my dead heart. He had removed a beautiful flower from my life and replaced it with another beautiful flower. Our wedding service was a celebration of that miracle. No matter what we faced in the future, we would stand firm in knowing that God had brought the two of us together.

11

The God of Comfort

Since that celebration day in 1978, God has continued to bless the Thorntons. I feel a little like Job must have felt when, after all his vast fortune and his health and his ten children were taken from him, he saw God and uttered, "I know that Thou canst do all things, and that no purpose of Thine can be thwarted."[1] And then God "restored the fortunes of Job"[2] and "The Lord blessed the latter days of Job more than his beginning."[3]   That's not to say there haven't been trials. I had to suffer the loss of an entire season when I had two operations on my right knee. There were other injuries that kept me out of action much of a second season, plus stinging criticism in print from a former teammate who felt that my faith was a detriment to the team. And there were attacks from others whom I thought understood me and what I stand for.

In our home, there were further trials as Gail and I had to adjust to marriage. None of them were major problems, but they had to be dealt with so that they would not become any bigger. Some of those adjustments could not have been anticipated before our marriage. But we agree that it was good we did not know them, for they might have discouraged us when God intended them to be blessings that would draw us closer together as a couple and a family.

Through all our trials, God has proved faithful. He has opened up vistas of ministry that we could not have imagined. Early in my baseball career I felt like an apprentice, eager to play just a small part in God's great work. But now we've been given greater opportunities to praise him and serve him, both in Cleveland and throughout the United States.

I am humbled by the ministry that God has opened up to us. I realize that I am nothing special. I do not have any unique faith or vision. The grace that God made available to Andre Thornton is available to every believer in the Lord Jesus Christ, no matter what the situation. There is no easy way I could have endured the tragedy in my life without taking hold of the Lord and depending on Him to provide my every need.

There may be a few people who are disappointed with my story. I've had some tell me that it would be more dramatic if in the midst of my grief I had cursed God. Perhaps it would have made better copy if I had had many questions and had eventually come through to find God and the answers. People have asked me, "I know you prayed and read the Bible, but what else did you do?" There was nothing else. What else could possibly add to what God was doing in my life? Until He brought Gail to me, He was my sole source of strength. Some people seem disappointed that it was so simple.

My messasge *is* simple: I have been through the darkest valley, and I was not forsaken. I was assailed by pounding waves and a violent storm, but my God never left me alone. My message is that God can give strength and peace and mercy through the worst of circumstances.

I did not ask to endure the death of my wife and daughter. I certainly would have been content to live the rest of my days with them. Yet God saw fit to call two of his dear children home. I had to trust Him in that. Never could I have imagined the impact that would be made through those two precious lives.

Hopefully, readers of this book will find my story an encouragement. The message can be summa-

Ron Kuntz

Roughing it up a bit with Andy.

Special moments with my son.

rized in this statement: God is faithful. He has proved His faithfulness to me in the greatest of need, and I believe He is capable of handling any other trial I might face. There is nothing too big for Him.

The only reason I look back now is to review again how good the Lord was to me. I can start back in Fort Dix, when He heard my simple prayer and began a new life in me. I can rejoice in the seven years that God gave to Gert and me together. I can thank Him for the peace and sense of His presence in that emergency room, when the nurses told me the tragic news. I can reflect on the week that followed, and how in the midst of grief He gave me the strength to be a witness to people around me. Even today, people still remember that funeral service at which I shared the hope we have in Christ.

Those weeks following the accident were special times when God was so incredibly real to me that I was immersed in His love and physically felt His healing power. Every word of Scripture was alive and meant for me during those days. Prayer took on a newer, deeper dimension. And then I could look back and see how God answered every one of my many prayers—for Andy's well-being, for answers to questions, for the ministry that this would have in the lives of others, and most of all for a new friend and wife.

I can rejoice at how God, in His perfect timing, provided just the right woman to become my new wife, and how he took us over the rocky road of adjustment and smoothed it out, allowing us to unite quickly into one. Then He gave us an addition to our family on January 4, 1981, when Gail gave birth to Jonathan David Thornton.

Perhaps the Apostle Paul sums up my feelings better than I can: "Blessed be the God and Father of our Lord Jesus Christ, the Father of mercies and God of all comfort, who comforts us in all our affliction

Gail, Jonathan, Andy and Andre:
Celebration of God's Miracle

so that we may be able to comfort those who are in any affliction with the comfort with which we ourselves are comforted by God. For just as the sufferings of Christ are ours in abundance, so also our comfort is abundant through Christ.'' (2 Corinthians 1:3-5 NASB).

Scripture References

1. Job 42:2 NASB.
2. Job 42:10 NASB.
3. Job 42:12 NASB.